RESTORED RECYCLED REMADE

Letters and stories of renewal

Thanks

Many thanks to my fellow authors – Alli, Dennis, Dick, Dinah, Mo, Oredola, Thomas and TJ – for their support and encouragement; and to Matt for his invaluable guidance. This book would not have been finished without your help. Also to Barbara, Jan and Stephen for being willing to read my outpourings and provide feedback and editing when needed.

Contents

Introduction

Restored

Chapter 1   Andrew

Chapter 2   School Daze

Chapter 3   Other People

Chapter 4   Simon's Story

Recycled

Chapter 5   Into the Wilderness

Chapter 6   Forget-Me-Not

Chapter 7   Burglar Bill

Chapter 8   Joseph's Story

Remade

Chapter 9   In Search of God's Will

Chapter 10   Church

Chapter 11   Dear Reader

Chapter 12   Saul's Story

Resources Page

GILL TAGGART

Introduction

Upcycling has recently become popular. There are books and television programmes about rescuing damaged, unwanted items or even a house and vehicle restoration, rebuilding or repurposing. It's all about making something from nothing; treasure from trash.

It may be that all that's needed is a good wash or clean up; remove the rust, lick of paint, apply a varnish or wax. It may be that dents need to be bashed out or surfaces sanded down. It could be that a complete rebuild is needed. Restoration can be tough. The experts make it look effortless, but we may find it easier just to cover dents, stains and problems with paint.

Sometimes we, too, can become damaged or broken by life. We may be dented by the pain of illness or bereavement, hidden under the weight of painful memories or other people's expectations.

Sometimes we, too, need to be restored, revitalised or remade.

I don't know what hurts you have in your life, and I'm not qualified to tell you how they can be healed or overcome. But as a Christian, I believe that God can heal, restore and make us new. Whether or not you share that belief, you still have the right to become the person you were made to be.

There are three sections to this book. Each section contains three letters, written to difficult circumstances, or people, in my past. Maybe you will be able to relate. Each contains a few thoughts on how we, or our circumstances, can be restored, revitalised or remade. Maybe you will find them helpful.

The final chapter in each section is a true story: the story of a Bible character who was made new, restored by God or who found himself in the dark and difficult places.

Restored

I know I will see you again one day.

Chapter 1
Andrew

Dear Andrew,

It's been so long; where do I start? Do you know how many times I've wished I could contact you, speak to you and have you back in my life? There are so many things I've wanted to tell you. So many questions I'd like you to answer.

And here's the first one: What did you have to go and die for?

Oh I know that's a silly question, it's not like you wanted or planned to leave us. At the age of twenty-two months you didn't understand the concept of death; you hadn't even begun to live.

We didn't have much time together, yet I do have some memories of you, Andrew.

One memory that I suspect will never quite go away is that of your final day. But more about that later.

You were born on 28 February; a few more hours and it would have been 29 February. No, I don't remember that. I was only two and a half then – give me a break.

You were the first of four boys born to mum and dad and my oldest brother.

All your photos were taken down after you died, but not thrown away. I have a few and I was later given some others. Do you want to see them? Yes, well you probably already have by now, but bear with me.

Here's one of Mum holding you in what looks like, your christening gown taken at our home in Bickley. Another is of Dad, holding you up and laughing; possibly about to throw you into the air. There is another one of me peering into your pram, which I vaguely recall. At least, I think I do! It's hard to tell sometimes. Mum would occasionally put your pram outside on the drive so you could sleep in the fresh air. At other times we would sit and play on a blanket on the front lawn. I've got a photo of that too.

This is one of my favourite photos; us in the park, sitting on the edge of the boating pond. I showed it to a school friend many years ago and she said that we looked like twins! Several years later that pond was drained and filled in, which caused another pang of grief when I went back and saw it. It's funny how some things just hit you, isn't it?

Our aunt gave me some photos, which I don't remember at all, involving the beach at Birchington, where Dad's parents settled when they retired. I loved that beach. I don't remember you being there, though obviously you were. In another lovely photo, that I wish I remembered, we were being introduced to our new baby brother. You looked quite chuffed to be a big brother. *

One of the memories that I have of you involved photographs:

We went to Bromley to have our photos taken in a studio above a shop. There were three or four pictures taken, yet only one seems to have survived, and I still have it. Because all your photos were hidden away, it was years before I came across it. I was glad to find it; even if it was a while before I was able to look at it. Anyway, that day I was wearing my red, knitted dress with the pom-poms. It's a black and white photograph but, trust me, it was red. You were wearing a short sleeved, white shirt with a navy blue collar and navy shorts. You weren't too happy, I recall, although you'd just clambered up the studio stairs on your own – so maybe that was it. You were certainly all smiles for the camera. I bet the photographer was a woman – you little flirt, you!

The second memory that I have of you involved stairs; the stairs at our home in Bickley. You had just fallen down them. Full of sisterly concern, I looked on and did nothing. Actually, I felt rather cross. I'd fallen down those same stairs a short time before and received lots of parental fuss, sweets etc. For some reason, I was sure you were copying me. "He just wants sweets," I thought, not considering for one moment that it was a very painful way of getting them. Sorry about that. In my defence, I was only four.

I'm sure you cried that day and at other times. Yet in most of the photos I have you are smiling or laughing. It's so lovely to see; yet it makes it harder in some ways. You had no idea what was about to happen.

None of us did.

On that final day, about a month before your second birthday, you had a sore throat. The doctor had been in that morning. Later in the day, he came back, and I wondered why. I was taken into the dining room with Mum, while Dad and the doctor went off into the front room where you were. I was playing and probably chattering away. But I think, even then, I could sense that mum wasn't really paying much attention to me. She was distracted; listening out in case Dad or the doctor needed her. I remember that when Dad did call for her, she told me to "stay there and play with your toys."

What I don't think anyone realised, though, was that I didn't stay and play. I wanted to know what was happening. So, I crept out of the room behind mum but stayed close to the opposite wall where I couldn't be seen. My last memory was of the three adults standing in a huddle in the hallway. Mum had her back to me but I think she was probably crying.

I couldn't tell you what happened after that, though it's possible that you could tell me. The following year of my life was almost a complete blank. I imagine that, today, it would be called "traumatic amnesia," or something. Personally, I think I'm rather glad of it. I was told that our grandparents wouldn't let us, or our cousins, go to your funeral. I'm not surprised. Our distraught parents had enough to cope with, without having a four year old and a six month old to look after.

I was at a Christian healing centre some years ago and remember being told that I needed to forgive our grandparents for that. I don't know why; it's never been an issue. They did what they felt was best and I never felt angry about it. I don't know, back then, if much was known about children and grief. They may have thought it unnecessary for us to go; that we were too young to understand. Probably they just wanted to protect us. A friend and I were once taken to the beach for the day because Grandma's neighbour had died and we were to be out of the way before the hearse arrived at the house. When other grandparents died I was told that funerals "weren't the place for little girls." Or simply that the deceased "wouldn't have wanted it." I was twenty before I first went to a funeral.

So even if I'd been able to go that day, Andrew, I wouldn't have been able to say "goodbye"; never mind to grieve.

It was many years before I was able to do that. There were, by then, a whole range of resources available: books on bereavement, counselling organisations, memory boxes, memorial services and so on.

But it felt different.

We are told that we can "get over" a bereavement after a certain length of time; there's an expectation that we will move on. In fact, eventually, this will begin to happen; it's healthy. If it doesn't appear to be happening, concerned relatives or professionals may begin to talk about being "stuck" in the grief cycle and recommend help or intervention. I would say this was probably what happened to Queen Victoria. She couldn't come to terms with Albert's death. Everything, at least for a while, was as he left it and she tried to carry out whatever he had planned. It was said that if she used the phrase "he wished it" there was no sense in discussing it. Victoria would shut herself away for months at a time, refusing to be seen in public, or, if she did appear, always wearing black. It seemed that she almost idolised her grief.

But what happens when the bereavement is long past but the emotions are present, raw and very painful? How do you tell people that something which happened nearly fifty years previously is as painfully real as if it had happened yesterday? How do you answer people who say "time heals" when it hasn't?

How can you get answers when there may not be anyone around to give them?

How can I talk and try to keep your memory alive, when there is almost no one around now who remembers you?

I know I will see you again one day. But, as I said, I have questions such as, "When I see you, will you be the same age as you were when you left us?" If so, that might be kind of strange, as our youngest great nephew is older than that. But if not, that means that you are currently in your late fifties, so how on earth will I recognise you? And will our brothers, two of whom never met you, know who you are?

In heaven, can you see people who are still on earth? Can you see me and what I've been doing over the years? Have you ever wished that you could comfort, or help, me? Do you know about our family: the nephews, nieces and great nephews? Are you with Dad and our grandparents now? Why couldn't you have sent me a sister?

Strangely, I think it was only after I became a Christian that all these questions, and doubts, really began. Maybe it was learning that Jesus performed miracles, helped people in trouble and even brought a few of them back to life again, that started me wondering. I remember being in a Bible study once, not that many years ago, actually, and hearing how Mary and Martha had both said to Jesus, "Lord, if you had been here, my brother would not have died." I understand that as a human being, Jesus couldn't have been in two places at once. But it hurt. Because

Jesus *was* with us all those years ago, in our house with me, with you and with our distraught parents. Yet, you still died.

Why?

The anguished howl that has echoed down the centuries.

Why me?

Why us?

Why you?

What was the purpose of your life, the little there was of it?

I tried for years to find the answer to that last question and some people, wanting to give comfort, have tried to provide one. Such as: "Maybe Andrew would have grown up to become a drug addict/alcoholic/have a terminal illness. Maybe God wanted to spare him all that." Well, possibly. But maybe you would have grown up to be a vicar, missionary or evangelist or make a fantastic contribution to politics, education or medicine. What about that? And I think we would rather have had you still here on earth – even ill, or addicted – as a brother, son, nephew, grandson, uncle and maybe father.

Some have said, "It wasn't God's plan or doing; it just happened. But He will bring good from it."
I don't know. Can good come from the death of a child? It may have come, in a way, if I had become a children's nurse, child bereavement counsellor or founded a charity in your name. Then at least the experience wouldn't have been wasted. But none of that happened.

And what about those who never got over the fact that you left us; like our grandmother who, afterwards, told the vicar that she'd lost her faith. Or our parents who barely spoke of you again. Or the fact that I spent several years feeling sad and traumatised. Or that our dad and grandparents died without finding peace; what about that?

Then there has sometimes been the "standard" Christian answer to the question of suffering, one which, I dare say, I have even used myself that, sadly, we live in a fallen world. Sickness and death came into the world the same time as sin, and Christians aren't exempt from suffering.

That is true, although it doesn't answer the question or take away any of the pain.

How can we be restored in bereavement?

I'm not sure that we can, not if restoration means having our loved ones back so that we can carry on and remain the same people that we were before.

The loss of someone who has been important to us, whom we have loved and who has loved, helped, taught us and moulded our lives is bound to affect and change us. Would we find comfort and healing if we had answers? Why do innocent children die before their parents? Why are health-conscious people struck down while others break all the health "rules" yet live to an old age? Why do good, hard-working, loving people die; yet others, who may waste their lives, misuse them or spend their time thinking up ways to do harm, live to a ripe old age? But no answer, however logical or compassionate, will ever bring back our loved ones. No "answer" could satisfy me, or my family and make your death all right.

Yet we are often restored, and find healing, through kindness: the love, thoughtful actions and consoling words of others. We may find healing by being kind to ourselves and giving ourselves time and permission to grieve, talk, shout, cry and heal. Also, for me, there is comfort in knowing that God understands. He understands my questions, my pain and the impact that your death had on my life. He understands because He's been there, done that, bought and worn the t-shirt. God has a Son who not only died but allowed Himself to be killed.

"Why have You abandoned Me?" Jesus whispered to (or maybe screamed at) God as He hung on the cross waiting to die. And His Father did nothing to help.

Yet, Jesus was raised from the dead. He has come out the other side. He has given us hope that death is not the end; that love is stronger.

It's time to bring this letter to an end.

It's a bit late to say, "sleep tight, little brother" and I'm not going to say goodbye, because in many ways you are still with me.

But until we meet again,

Your big sister,

Gill

To see these pictures, go to my website:
www.restoredrecycledremade.com

Achievements and exam results don't define who you are.

Chapter 2
School Daze

Dear eleven-year-old Gill,

Congratulations on getting into your first choice of secondary school.

You will learn a lot during the next six years or so. Some of it will be enjoyable, interesting and relevant for your future; some of it less so.

I wish I'd been able to give you this letter all those years ago. You might not have believed me, taken any notice or been able to change anything but at least you might have been a little more prepared for life at Beaverwood.

Firstly, it seems that you've been getting a lot of colds recently.

Any day now, the doctor will suggest that maybe it's something else and you will be sent for tests. These will show that you have a number of environmental allergies: dust, dust mite, grass pollen, feathers, wool and a few more. You will begin taking the first of many tablets and an eighteen-week course of injections. These will be a bit of a pain – quite literally – as well the fact that the course will be repeated for the next three years. There's nothing to worry about, although you will feel irritated and embarrassed at the constant sneezing and the fact that you feel "different" to others. Try not to be. It will be a dreadful nuisance in the summer, as the powers that be decide that the best time of the year to hold important exams is in the hay-fever season. But at least others get hay-fever, too, so there will be some understanding and empathy.

The most important thing to remember about these allergies is that they're not some kind of punishment. They will be debilitating and distressing, and it's absolutely OK to go to the doctors and to healing services to try to be free from them. But you'll find it a lot easier if you can learn that you're not going to be exempt from problems just because you're a Christian. I know you'd like to be able to say to people that having faith and being a Christian means that you won't have any problems, but that's not the case. Feeling ill, depressed or overwhelmed isn't a reflection on your faith; though there are Christians who might say otherwise. You'll save yourself a lot of hassle if you can get rid of and refuse to entertain those ideas. Faith isn't some kind of insurance policy and God doesn't owe you any favours just because you believe in Him.

So, school! You will be told that school is about "getting an education." But, at this stage, it is really all about studying a number of subjects to a certain point, taking exams and passing them. You will then get a certificate to show which subjects you have passed and may be led to believe that if you don't have this then you aren't very competent in that area. This is nonsense!

Firstly, there's so much in life that is educational: hobbies, travelling and visiting historical places and reading books. You'll also love biographies; read books such as 'The Cross and the Switchblade' and learn of the author's work with teenage drug addicts in America. Through reading 'God's Smuggler' you will learn about countries where Christians are persecuted for their faith. Through reading books by Corrie Ten Boom or Anne Franks you will learn of how Jews were persecuted for theirs. But these don't appear on a school syllabus and won't be reckoned as important. The only thing that seems to matter is passing exams. Someone with ten O-levels is more likely to get job interviews than someone with four. The person with ten O-levels will feel, or be told, that they're a success, that they are better or more worthy. The person with four may feel that they have failed or are worthless. The person with ten O-levels may feel that they have to push themselves even harder and maintain that success because that is what is expected of them. While the person with four might give up trying. To be fair, few people can walk into a job with no qualifications at all and the more exams you pass, the more options you'll have. But lots of good exam results will also make the school look good, ensure that standards are kept up and that they receive lots of pupils the following year.

Even at this age, the message seems to be "you are what you have achieved."

Another reason why the emphasis on exams is all wrong is that people learn in different ways at different paces. You will discover, years later, that you are an activist and that you learn by doing. You will also be keen to learn those things that interest you but not so much otherwise. So if someone took you to the seaside, left you to explore rock pools and then asked you to write a project on the different types of seaweed, find out why a crab walks sideways or how a pearl is made, you wouldn't have any trouble in doing so and would doubtless get a decent mark for it. But because seashore life isn't on the syllabus and biology will involve sitting in a classroom learning about the life cycle of the amoeba, you will have little interest in it. You will later be judged to be "not good at biology."

If they want you to learn, they should teach something interesting and relevant. In history lessons, you'll have to study the two World Wars, but won't learn much about the history of your own country. In geography, you will learn how to draw contour lines in a sandpit, but won't learn how to get to Lewisham by bus or where your home town of Bromley is on a map of the UK (Hint: Don't put it in the middle.).

In fact, you will have to take subjects that you have no interest in or aptitude for, although you may later choose to give some of them up. This is apparently supposed to be character-forming: "We all have to do things that we don't like." But you'd think that an establishment which places so much emphasis on achievements would want to help you shine. And your time to shine won't be in a classroom learning things you don't want to learn, I'm afraid. In a way, that makes it difficult to learn – but that's OK! Dad was right: the important thing is that you do your best. Achievements and exam results don't define who you are.

Sadly, you won't learn that lesson just yet. The school environment you are in won't help with that; with its emphasis on achievements. Maybe that's why some of the teachers will insist on reading out test results in descending order: to try to shame people into doing better and moving up a place next time.

Despite all this, you will pass a decent number of O-levels and you will go into the sixth form to begin A-levels.

I'd like to tell you not to bother with these: you're going to end up in nursing and you won't need them. In the future, that will all change and nursing will require higher qualifications and be more classroom-based. This is a shame because exams are not needed to be able to show compassion, warmth and empathy. Nursing is one of the professions where who you are is more important than what you know. I suppose that, as you won't actually know what you want to do in the future, A-levels and university might actually have given you more options.

It might have been good to stay on at school and study subjects that interested you, without the pressure of an exam at the end of it, which is possible at evening classes. But that's not how it works. Teachers are there to do a job, which involves getting you through exams to university. Then you can study and do more exams and get a degree, which may or may not be useful to you in years to come.

Parents and teachers will persuade you that this is the best, and maybe only, path that you can take: the only way to get a good education. So you will try to follow it, even though you would rather not.

You'll join some interesting clubs at school and will make some good friends, though it'll take a while. No one can get on with, like or be popular with everyone, but there will be some in your class who will make a point of teasing and opposing you. No doubt they will call it "fun," "banter" or "a bit of a laugh." I call it bullying.

Oh, I realise that, compared to what some kids went through, it's nothing. It won't be physical and, thankfully, knives and weapons weren't an issue back then (or not in our "respectable girls' school" anyway). But mocking, belittling and hurting someone just for the fun of it – because you feel that they are different/inferior to you and deserve it – is not on.

I sometimes wonder whether any of those girls married and had children who later got bullied. I wonder if, as they attempted to soothe them and dry their tears, they remembered their own behaviour at school? Or if any of them had been brave enough to admit that they had thought that teasing, picking on others and making them unhappy was a bit of a laugh? I wonder if any of them went on to become teachers and taught about inclusivity, diversity and respect? If they gave lectures about bad behaviour or dished out punishments to children who were unkind, did they have a twinge of conscience?

Some people who were bullied at school use it to explain a life of crime or why they may have gone off the rails. Being bullied may well have led to a lack of self-esteem or a desire to hurt the people who were supposed to have protected them. Being bullied may well happen because the bullies themselves grew up with it and it's all they know. Someone who has been bullied might use the experience to set up a charity to help others. They might be prompted to follow a certain career so that others won't suffer as they did. But I've never heard anyone saying, "I understand how bullies think because I used to be one. I want to stop people from becoming as I was."

I can't tell you why those girls will act the way that they will. I'd like to say jealousy, but I very much doubt it. Maybe it's insecurity; the only way they can feel better about themselves is to make others feel bad. Maybe they think that having a joke at someone else's expense will give some sort of credibility and status. If social media had been around then, they may have contented themselves with posting pictures of pop groups and getting "likes." Then again, social media will, in the future, make bullying, and a number of other things, worse. At least the name calling will be done by a few sad individuals and confined to school – not plastered over the internet for anyone to comment on or laugh at under the cloak of anonymity.

I'd like to say that dealing with bullies at school will give you the tools and confidence for dealing with adults who are bullies. But, sadly, I don't think that will happen.

There isn't much that I regret in my life but I do wish that my school days had been different. I wish, Gill, that you could have been encouraged to learn in your own way, at your own pace. I wish that you'd been able to decide what you wanted to do when you left school. I wish that you'd been able to stand up to, or at least had an answer for, the school bullies.

If I was able to give you any advice, I'd say that I'd like you to be yourself. You'll have to conform to some extent with the uniform and school rules, but try not to compromise, give in or do things just to make other people, including your parents, happy. It doesn't matter if some girls tease or don't like you – that's their problem and loss. You're better than they are – not simply because you'll get good grades in French and they will be desperate to copy your homework.

Enjoy and work at the things you can and leave the others behind. Stand up for what you believe; you have a right to believe it. Be kind to yourself and have a bit more confidence in your abilities (I'll get back on you on that one.).

You're not perfect, and never will be, but you have the right to be the person that God made you to be.

Take care of yourself,

A slightly older Gill

RESTORED RECYCLED REMADE

I love it when someone, who has been put down by other people, written off and told that they won't amount to much, succeeds.

Chapter 3
Other People

Dear Other People,

You have been around for my whole life and many, many years before. Most of the time, I'm very glad that you're around. I don't think I'd be here if you weren't. Other people brought me into this world – no easy task, I'm told. Other people made all the clothes I've ever worn, made my food, educated me, gave me work, patched up my cuts and bruises and cut my hair.

Other people have taught me about my faith, the world around me and how to apply my faith to the world around me. I need you in my life; most of us need you in our lives. Way back in the Garden of Eden we read "It is not good for man to be alone" (Genesis 2:18). We were born to be with others, to be in a family or community. We all enjoy our own company at times, some more than others, but you're good to have around.

A lot of things are easier if we have other people in our lives. We can feel safer. Neighbourhood watch schemes only work if a group of people are looking out for each other. We have friends, companions and maybe even a purpose in life. How many older people may feel isolated because they've retired? Or because their children have moved away, are at work or are otherwise busy with their own lives? How many may become ill, isolated or even take their own lives because they're alone and feel they have no purpose? We can often achieve many more things in life if we have other people to help us, to offer their gifts, strengths and encouragement. Many hands make light work and all that. Marathon runners have sometimes said that at a point when they were flagging, it was the encouragement of the crowd that spurred them on or that there was a team of them running for their chosen charity or cause and they trained and ran together.

It should be said that some people don't want to have you in their lives through choice. Some people may have Asperger's, autism or some other condition and it distresses them to have you around. Generally, though, it's good that you're there to provide company, friendship and comfort. There are many stories and illustrations about the value of teamwork.

But as much as I love having you in my life, Other People, you do tend to interfere too much and have too much influence. In particular, you sometimes need to keep your opinions to yourself. I know that might sound ungrateful and at times we all need a second opinion, an unbiased view, a word of advice or counsel. But, sometimes, this goes too far and we may feel that you're beginning to take over our lives.

The problem may start as early as our school days when we're introduced to one of your relatives: *"everyone."* How often have we heard children say, "But *everyone* has got a phone"; *"Everyone else* will be going"; *"Everyone* wears make up, trainers or a certain brand of clothing"? I don't think this is usually said maliciously or from a desire to get their own way. Maybe it comes from the fear of losing out or being seen as the odd one out, which seems to be one of the things that can lead to bullying. But it could be a subtle form of coercion and parents give in and buy the possession or agree to the outing in question so that their child won't miss out. Their child wants to be like other people.

We might think that by the time we reach adulthood we would know better. I have felt that people sometimes pay lip service to the idea that we're all individuals, that we need to find our own way and do what's right for us rather than follow the crowd. But the reality is often different. Society is made up of other people. New trends, fashions and behaviours begin to emerge because enough of these other people declare that something should be so. A product is manufactured and promoted; advertisers play on the fact that we want to be in with the crowd or need to keep up with the Joneses. New fashion is released every year. Hemlines are up, then they're down. Purple is a no-go one year, then it's all the rage. Some people spend a fortune because they have to have the latest garment that everyone is wearing. Why? Because other people have decided that this is what the thing is going to be this year and there's pressure, partly through advertising and partly through the media, to conform. A few years ago on the TV show 'Great British Sewing Bee' it was announced that the contestants were going to make new garments from old clothes because we throw away an obscene amount of clothing and we need to start recycling them. A lot of people may give to charity shops instead of throwing things away. However, I wonder how much of the discarding is the fault of the fashion industry?

It's the same with possessions: There have been stories of people queuing all night outside a toy shop so that their children have the latest toy, phone, trainers or whatever for Christmas. Which brings us back to the "everyone's got it" syndrome!

Morals can also be changed or adopted because other people start behaving in a certain way. It wasn't that many years ago that sex before marriage was frowned upon. It happened, of course. The problem pages of my teenage magazines sometimes contained letters from girls who had given in to this temptation and were scared of being found out. Pregnant women were sent away, secretly or in disgrace, to have their babies. In one case I know of a woman who was put into an institution for people with learning difficulties, partly for that reason. It was as if having one child out of wedlock was disgraceful; but to have two suggested that the woman had some kind of mental deficiency.

Nowadays and sadly (in my view), sex before marriage is almost the norm. Teenage pregnancy seems to be more common and the problem pages of magazines have letters from people who feel there is something wrong with them because they haven't slept with anyone else. Why the change? I know nothing really about trends in society or the reasons for those trends. But surely at some point it would have started with someone or a group of people who began to act differently?

Marital status and family life may also be affected by what other people think. When I was single I was sometimes asked when I was going to find a boyfriend. Not by parents, I hasten to add, but by strangers or casual friends who felt they had a right to steer the course of my life. When I was married, the question was, "When are you going to have children?" I've known some couples who had a child and were asked when they were going to have another one and some who had only girls and were asked if they were going to try for a boy. Sometimes, women who have a boy and then go on to have a girl, will say their family is "complete" even if they do have further children later. Why? Because society has decided that the ideal family is two parents, a son and a daughter.

In subtle and not so subtle ways, you seem to influence our lives, telling us how to live, what to wear, what to do and buy. You also sometimes try to tell us how to think or to act. This is very hard for children but even if we are adults, there may still be a part of us that wants to have parental approval.

I have heard people who say, for example, "My parents want me to study science, but all I really want to do is paint." Or "My dad wants me to follow in his footsteps and be a doctor, but I don't like science and I want to teach young children." I've witnessed situations where a child is told to study a subject because their parents want them to do it. But either their heart isn't in it or they struggle with it and they fail. Then the parents are annoyed, especially if they're paying for their child's education. And the child might feel they have failed to be and do what their parents want them to be or do.

I'm sorry to say, also, but as well as having too much influence, not keeping your opinions to yourself and trying to persuade me to change my life for you, you also tend to judge by appearances.

I have mentioned that I used to have ME. This is an invisible illness which, like a number of others – epilepsy, diabetes, heart problems, mental health issues and so on – can't be seen. Most of the time, therefore, if I managed to get out and about, I looked OK and other people couldn't always understand, or did not always believe that anything was wrong. My GP refused to believe me when I said that I was unable to walk to her surgery for an appointment. Not everyone was like this, of course. But I felt that some other people thought that I was lazy. I was once told that if I got out of bed and got a job, I wouldn't be so tired all the time. This person apologised when I explained, but it didn't stop her making a judgement based on what she could see.

Then I suffered a slipped disc which required surgery, resulted in nerve damage and which meant using crutches at first and then a walking stick. And I found that attitudes changed. My GP believed that I had a physical problem. She could see the result of it and had the doctor's notes and scans which confirmed it. I received benefits the first time I applied for them.

When I "just" had ME, I would either be ignored, asked why I was walking so slowly or occasionally received an unwarranted comment on my level of fitness. When I was hobbling along on crutches, people encouraged me.

When I started to use a walking stick, folk would sometimes comment on the colour, (I have six in various colours), or that it matched my outfit. My mobility scooter provoked questions and quips including, "Give us a lift!" or "Can I sit in your basket?"

Now that people can see that I have a mobility issue, most are lovely, encouraging and comment favourably on all the things that I'm able to do, or willing to try. Some have been bolder and asked me straight out about my disability: "Do you get arthritis?" "Have you had a hip or knee replacement?" This is often before telling me all about their arthritis, hip or knee replacements. Usually, I don't mind that at all. In fact, I have even tried to look on it as a ministry.

So, grateful as I am to have you in my life, Other People, I don't like the influence that you've had over me and how I've ended up doing what you wanted, instead of standing by my convictions or decisions (Though, to be fair, that is probably partly my fault for allowing you such power.).

I don't like it when you've judged by appearances. You do sometimes look silly when it's shown that you don't know what you're talking about. But you shouldn't make that judgement.

But I love it when you're proved wrong. I love it when someone, who has been put down by other people, written off and told that they won't amount to much, succeeds. An unknown sports star wins the top prize. The horse that never seemed to have had a chance, storms past the thoroughbreds to win the race. The pupil who sits at the back of the class and gets overlooked, or even picked on, gets the top grades in exams. One thing I've learned over the years is that if other people think or say that I won't be able to do something, that that's a good reason for trying (It doesn't always work, before you all rush to start reverse psychology on me.)!

Do I sound harsh saying that sometimes I hate it when other people influence us, judge us or prevent us from being the people we should be? Or that I'm pleased when these other people are proved wrong?

Maybe. But, you see, to you I'm an "other person" too.

Best wishes,

Gill

So, whatever mistakes you've made in your life, don't give up; there is hope of restoration.

Chapter 4
Simon's Story

My name is Simon. I'm a fisherman from Galilee, and I'd like to tell you the story of how my friend Jesus restored me after I messed up big time.

Fishing might not sound like much, but it's a good life. It was all I knew and it might have stayed that way for many years, had we not had an extraordinary meeting that one day.

It had been a disappointing night out on the lake: all that waiting, watching and hauling in of slippery nets and we caught nothing. As we were washing the nets the next morning, someone asked if he could borrow my boat for a while – just to sit in. I couldn't see any harm, so I agreed.

I had seen this man, Jesus, around, but hadn't spoken to Him. They said He was a teacher, and the things He was teaching about God were amazing and exciting. Centuries ago, our ancestors told of how they'd actually spoken with the God who made them; how they listened and were guided by and saw miracles from Him. Abraham, Moses and Elijah were all heroes of our faith. But many years later, there was no one who even talked about God anymore – until John the Baptiser came along. We thought God had probably abandoned us.

But was it possible that God had remembered us after all? Jesus certainly seemed to think so. The way He talked about God you'd think He was a close relative, or at least

His Best Friend. We took our time sorting the nets that morning so that we could listen to Him.

When He'd finished teaching, Jesus looked at me and said, "Go out again into deep water and throw your nets over the other side of the boat." That irritated me. He may have been a first rate teacher but He clearly knew nothing about our business. Yet something about His expression, the words I'd just heard from His lips and the desperation that comes from despair, led me to do what He said.

I wouldn't have believed the result if I hadn't seen it for myself. Fish... hundreds of fish! But it wasn't the size of the catch or the amount of money we could make that took my breath away. This was a miracle. This was the kind of thing God did – or used to do. I didn't know who this Jesus was but this was incredible and more than a little scary. Jesus was like one of the prophets that we used to have in Israel. I wasn't worthy even to be in His presence and yet, for some reason, He invited me, my brother Andrew and a few others to follow Him. He wanted me? After what I'd seen and heard, He didn't have to ask twice.

How could I begin to describe the events of the following few years? We saw miracles and sights that we couldn't have dreamed of. Ordinary water turned into the best wine; ordinary people were restored and given new hope. A crowd of people fed from a few loaves and fish; thousands more nourished with the news that God loved and cared for them. We were challenged, amazed, confused, delighted, rebuked and stretched in our beliefs, attitudes and in what we saw happening all around us. We inwardly cheered when Jesus confronted religious leaders and challenged stifling traditions. We inwardly cringed when He associated with the unclean, the sinful, the damaged and the hurt. It was an unbelievable time; one which, we assumed, and hoped, would go on forever.

I can't pinpoint exactly when things changed.

Maybe it was that occasion when Jesus asked us who we thought He was; a very good, and important, question. I was about to wax lyrical about his great healing ministry, teachings and insights and how lucky we were to have Him when, suddenly, I heard myself saying, "You are the Christ, the Son of God." I had no idea where that came from but Jesus told me that it had been revealed to me by God Himself. Then He gave me a new name, "Peter" meaning "rock" and said that this was the rock on which He would build His church.

But before we could take that in, or dwell on it, Jesus said something else: that He was going to die. Now, that was confusing; everyone knew the Messiah couldn't die. I told Jesus that this couldn't be allowed. But then I was in trouble for making such a suggestion. Jesus stated that He was going to be badly treated, to suffer at the hands of the priests and elders and be rejected by them. Reject Him? They were more likely to want to crown Him. Our Messiah was here! You may not be able to imagine just how important that news was to a Jew. Most of us had spent our lives waiting and hoping for the Messiah. The leaders would be delighted when we told them that He was here. This news would electrify Israel; we would be set free from those tiresome Romans and be able to live as God's people. Yet, we weren't allowed to tell anyone.

We didn't understand.

There isn't really enough space to tell you of other events of the next few months: the incredible mountain top experience; Jesus' insistence that He had to go to Jerusalem; His arrival on the back of a donkey; how He overturned tables in the temple and drove out money lenders or how He cursed a fig tree. This was a side to Jesus I hadn't really seen before: purposeful. It's almost as though He wanted to court controversy.

It was nearly time for the Passover. One of the most important festivals for a Jew, it was a reminder of the time when we'd been slaves in Egypt and God had sent Moses to rescue us so that we could worship God and be the people He made us to be.

Jesus had arranged for us to go to a certain room so that we could celebrate this important feast together. But we soon discovered that this would be no ordinary Passover meal. There was nothing wrong with the food but where was the story of our deliverance from Egypt? Or how the Hebrew slaves had been saved from death by the blood of a lamb? Why did Jesus take bread and say, "Do this in memory of Me"? Do what in memory of Him? Why would He say that?

It seemed, also, that one of the preparations for the meal had been overlooked. It was customary for a host to provide a slave to wash guests' dirty, dusty feet. No one had thought of this, so Jesus chose to do it Himself; our Master and Rabbi washing our feet – how embarrassing! I didn't want Him to lower Himself like that and, at first, wouldn't let Him wash my feet. But Jesus said that not only was it right for Him to do so but if I didn't let Him wash my feet I couldn't belong to Him, for some reason.

Of course, I allowed Him to then but I didn't understand why. It was a confusing thing.

Then there was Judas. I don't know what had gotten into him but it seemed there was something he had to do urgently. How rude! Why couldn't he have waited?

Jesus had already spoken of betrayal – another confusing thing – and didn't seem too surprised that Judas was leaving. But it was odd.

Jesus had also told us that I was going to deny Him. I really don't know why He was suddenly saying these weird things, but it was ridiculous. "No, of course I won't," I replied. "Other people might, but not me." How could Jesus think that I could let Him down like that? He had called me a rock; He must have known He could depend on me. Jesus didn't argue the point, though, and after a few more encouraging, comforting but puzzling words, we sang a hymn and went out.

I don't know why we even did that; it was way after sunset, and we could easily have slept in that room until morning. But, no, we went to a garden called Gethsemane.

Once there, Jesus took me, James and John to one side and told us to wait, watch and to pray for Him. Well, we would have, even though we had no idea what we were watching or praying for. But it was late, we had eaten food and drunk wine and I, for one, was worn out with all the confusion, questions and conflicting emotions of the last few hours.

We fell asleep.

The next thing we knew we were surrounded by soldiers. Was that Judas I saw with them? He went up to Jesus, greeted Him like an old friend and kissed Him.

Then the soldiers surged forward and took Jesus away.

What...?

I started hitting out blindly with my sword and sliced the ear of one of the guards. But they wouldn't let go of Jesus and I could only follow, at a distance.

I followed Him just as far as the courtyard but could go no further. I was frozen, physically and mentally you might say. I was standing next to a charcoal fire trying to get warm when it happened: A young servant girl asked me if I was with Jesus.

"I don't know what you're talking about," I said, hardly able to believe the words that had just come from my mouth. I tried to walk away, but she followed me. "He's one of them," she told the gathered crowd. What could I do? I had just said that she was talking nonsense, I could hardly now say, "I've just remembered, I do know Him." There was only one answer I could give: "No, I'm definitely not."

A little later, someone else said, "You're not from round here; you have a Galilean accent. You must be one of those who was with that Jesus bloke." I was terrified. They'd found me out. All they needed to do was to call over to one of the Roman soldiers and that would have been it for me. I felt I was in danger. I was thoughtless, stupid. But I could do nothing for Jesus now, so did it matter? Whatever I said wouldn't help Him but I could still have a good life if I wasn't arrested. I just had to convince them.

Jesus was being taken across the courtyard just as I finished my little outburst and He turned and looked at me. He wasn't angry, He just looked sad and rather disappointed. That made me feel uncomfortable. But just then, the cock crowed and I remembered what He had said. I was devastated. At that moment I was the least rock-like person you could imagine.

Almost the last thing I had said to Jesus before His arrest was, "Of course I won't deny you." Now He was being led away – quite possibly to His death – and I'd denied Him. What if those were my final words to Him? What if I never got a chance to explain?

Things moved with depressing speed after that.

Jesus' "trial" was held at night, so it was illegal. Nevertheless, He was found guilty and crucified. The lads and I ran off and shut ourselves in a room. We were safe, thanks to the locks and bolts on the door, yet were imprisoned by fear, guilt and sadness. What had the last three years been all about? Why were we led to hope that God's kingdom had come, only for it to be snatched away by pagans?

Jesus had saved and helped so many others. Why was He not able to save or help Himself? Where was His miracle?

After a few days, I decided to go fishing. I didn't know what else to do. We didn't catch anything of course – this was our punishment for letting Jesus down. It felt as though the empty nets symbolised my life; my former profession had gone and there was nothing to look forward to in the future.

Then someone on the shore told us to let our nets down on the other side of the boat. As if that would make a difference! But we had nothing to lose, so we did. I'm told that we hauled in 153 large fish.

Somewhere in the depths of my brain a memory was surfacing. This had happened before when Jesus called me to follow Him. Was it Him? I needed to see... indeed it was! I jumped out of the boat, forgetting my questions, fears and guilt. As I struggled up the beach, I could see and smell that Jesus had built a fire.

He had bread, was cooking some fish and invited us to come and eat. What was going on? None of us said much as we ate; what could we say? After breakfast Jesus said that He wanted to see me alone.

This was it. What was I going to say? How could I defend or explain myself?

As it happened, I didn't need to. Jesus spoke first and simply asked me if I loved Him. "Yes Lord," I replied, "You know how fond I am of You."

Jesus didn't comment but told me to feed His lambs. I was about to ask Him what He meant when He asked me again, "Simon, son of John, do you love Me?" Why was He calling me "Simon?" Had He taken away my new name? Was He saying that I wasn't rock-like after all and didn't deserve it? If He was angry with me, why was He telling me to feed His lambs?

He asked me a third time if I loved Him. Why was He doing this? I had said that I did; didn't He believe me? Then He invited me, again, to follow Him.

And I think I finally began to understand. I had denied Jesus three times and He asked me, three times, if I loved Him. Jesus restored and forgave me. I was important to Him. He wanted a relationship with me based on love, not guilt or duty, and He had a task for me to do.

So, whatever mistakes you've made in your life, don't give up; there is hope of restoration.

You can't have messed up as badly as I did, yet Jesus forgave me and gave me a second chance. He's good like that.

GILL TAGGART

Recycled

I began to look on this as a different kind of ministry.

Chapter 5
Into the Wilderness

Dear ME*

I always think of a wilderness as being a bleak, dry, barren, desolate place. Maybe it is. A wilderness wouldn't make it onto Trip Advisor's top ten list of holiday destinations. It's not a place to go for a day trip; it takes time to cross or explore.

Having any kind of long-term illness feels like time in a wilderness. Normal life is put on hold and plans delayed, while we focus on our condition and the relief of our symptoms.

Having you in my life, ME, was like that. I felt that I really ought to hate you and, at first, maybe I did. After several years of searching for a job or career, I started a three-year nursing course for people with learning disabilities. Finally, I had a calling like everybody else. And then you put a hold on that.

It was in the third year of my nurse's training that I started to feel uncommonly tired. That wasn't too surprising, I suppose. I was newly married, had moved house twice, had the responsibilities of a third year student nurse and finals were looming. I didn't confide in my tutors, anticipating hollow laughter, stories of "in my day" and a pep talk on getting more sleep or not burning the candle at both ends (as if).

This was not the usual type of weariness, though, it was different. I could function up to a point but then it was as if

50

I hit a proverbial brick wall, which was not eased by rest. After a few weeks of this, I went to the doctor's, got signed off sick and had blood tests, which showed nothing unusual. I rested, slept, felt stronger and went back to work. Yet within 24 hours, I had an overwhelming need to rest and sleep, wondered how much longer I could continue, ended up back at the GP and was signed off sick again.

It wasn't long before my tutors began to notice and express concern – not for me, but for the amount of time I was taking off from my course. We had certain subjects to cover before the final exams and were "allowed" twenty-eight days off sick over a period of just over three years. Any more than that and we would have needed to stay on for a few months after our finals. I was called in to the senior tutor's office because I had had "too many" sick days. All of which were legitimate, incidentally, unlike some of my fellow students who would take sick days to recover from hangovers or to go shopping. I was asked, reasonably enough, why I was having so much time off sick and said that I kept feeling very tired. I don't know what I expected this tutor to do; I had no answers myself.

I was taken aback when cautioned about possibly losing my friends, and even my new husband, if I continued to be, or claim to be, sick and tired. I was then asked if I needed help. I did; I needed a diagnosis. I didn't realise that this would lead to a call for a psychiatric referral. The following morning, this tutor delivered a class on counselling techniques. Had I been more assertive, I might have asked him if he thought that his actions of the previous evening were good counselling practice and, if not, why had he done that? I wish I had said that. As it was, I returned home and wrote a letter, resigning from the course for health reasons.

So ended my training and my career, and I left with nothing. Or, at least, with three years' worth of teaching and experience, but without the piece of paper that identified me as a Registered Nurse for the Mentally Handicapped.*

A friend of mine, a former nurse, once told me that, on average, it took four years to recover from ME. "I'm not going to have it for that long," I thought in disgust, completely forgetting that it was beyond my control. I was right about that. I didn't have you in my life for four years, but for eighteen. Eighteen years of loss: my career, my health, my hopes for the future. Eighteen years of trying to get answers from doctors, battling with benefit forms and claims and with people who didn't understand, and didn't try to. Eighteen years of limitations, frustration, boredom, new discoveries, new priorities and new ministries. But more about that later!

In some ways, I was fortunate. Through the ME magazines and a local group, I came to hear about people who had been so badly affected that they were in bed and had been for months, if not years. I met, or heard, about others who had been badly hit for a while, but after a couple of years of severe limitations had gotten better. I knew someone who, though moderately affected, needed to work and managed it by cutting out his social life and working flexible hours. Some had ME so badly that their lives were on hold. Others were using whatever energy they still had in caring for their children who were far too young to understand. I wasn't confined to bed or even to the house. In the early days, I could

52

even walk a fair distance, though I paid for it afterwards. That was the problem with this illness: I could function almost normally, up to a certain point. After that, I needed to rest and even sleep. Someone who met me for a short period of time, such as my GP, might have thought, "She seems to be doing OK." But they didn't see the aftermath; the price that I paid for pushing myself to keep going.

I once heard it explained in this way: Imagine that you have a handful of spoons, let's say twelve. Each spoon represents a unit of energy and they all represent your total amount of energy for the day. You will lose spoons as you complete various tasks, or activities. So, getting out of bed may only use a little energy, say one spoon. Getting ready may use two spoons or more. Walking downstairs, making a cup of tea and/or breakfast may use up another spoon. You could then be left with eight spoons to see you through the rest of the day. How are you going to use them? Collect your child from school or go to the doctors? Maybe you could go for a walk or to the shops. Have you allowed for the unexpected, such as the slow moving queue in the shop or bank?   Or the screaming child who may give you a headache? How many spoons will this excursion take? Two or four? If you choose to stay at home and read a book, the concentration needed may still use one spoon. And supposing the phone rings or a friend calls round? Social visits were a bit of a problem for me. There weren't that many of them and I was usually pleased to see people even if I knew that I wasn't up to a visit. Better to see them and suffer later than turn them away and risk them not returning. Then it will be lunchtime, which may cost at least another spoon.

An afternoon nap may then be a necessity. You won't get any spoons back but you shouldn't lose any either – unless you are interrupted by the phone or doorbell, that is. By teatime, you might have three of your twelve spoons left if you are lucky. How are you going to use these to cover your evening activities and bedtime routine? You can't "borrow" spoons from the following day, nor can you carry over any that are left. I used to try to save up my energy to be used on an activity or social event. But that's not possible because ME is very mean like that. So, if you hear a person who you know to be unwell talk about not having enough spoons they are probably referring to their energy levels, rather than requesting you go to Harrods to buy them some more cutlery.

This illustration applies to other illnesses besides ME.

The nature of this illness obviously made a number of things quite difficult, but also led to a lot of new discoveries. I joined a local ME group and later became its secretary. This involved learning things that I had not previously thought myself capable of doing, such as using a computer database. Computers were quite new to me then and took a lot of concentration. Even more surprising, then, that I should set up a website about this illness. It used a very basic programme and uploading to the internet was completely beyond me, but I did it. 'ME Matters' was born and launched on an unsuspecting world. I later added another, called 'ME Crafts', which described crafts that people with ME might be able to enjoy, even if confined to bed. Around this time, I also produced a booklet on ME which was accepted by a couple of doctor's surgeries and two local libraries. My own GP practice was one of those which accepted this booklet, yet my GP didn't believe in the illness.

I began counted cross stitch and dabbled with embroidery several years before I became ill. Now that I had an enforced period of rest, I thought it would be good to continue with these. But I soon found that a lot of effort and concentration was needed to produce anything worthwhile and that friends were having birthdays quicker than I could stitch the cards. I could, on reflection, have sent them a card for the previous birthday, thereby knocking a year off their age and guaranteeing lifelong friendship. But I didn't think of it at the time. I noticed an advert for a rubber stamping starter's kit in one of my cross stitch magazines. This looked interesting and it appeared it would be less effort. So, a new craft was born, or discovered, and it was considerably easier to make greetings cards in this way. Over the years I have explored other crafts with varying degrees of success, but I enjoy the whole creative process. I have recently started making greetings cards from packaging and recycled paper to show, and remind myself, that good, and even beauty, can come from rubbish.**

My former art and needlework teachers would no doubt have been astounded to realise that I was able to do anything at all in this area (I still have my junior school report as evidence).

I was disappointed that I wasn't able to pursue what I saw as a pastoral ministry. But I realised that I could show care in a new way: through a home-made card. I began to look on this as a different kind of ministry.

Another new and surprising discovery came after our move to Surrey. I found it was almost impossible to attend Sunday worship at our local Anglican church, so I joined the Methodists. A chance conversation led to a question about training as a Local (lay) Preacher. I'd never had a desire or intention to preach and told God this, so the idea was ridiculous. Yet the thought wouldn't go away and I felt I should try, even if it only meant I'd be vindicated if I should fail. I was licensed as a Local Preacher three years later. That was fifteen years ago.

I often refer to this time in my life as being in the wilderness. Was it bleak? Yes, often! Waking late each day, needing to sleep in the afternoons and still not having much energy, was tedious and discouraging. Was it dry? Yes, in terms of my career. Was it barren? Not really! The wilderness is a place with a different pace of life, but a place that offers time to be, to re-evaluate and to learn new skills. There is life in the wilderness. But we may have to look for it and it won't be what we're expecting. Neither was it desolate for me. I never looked on this as a punishment from God, quite simply because it wasn't. And He was with me in the boredom, frustration and so on. He gave me His "own dear presence to cheer and to guide"; certainly "strength for today" and often "bright hope for tomorrow."***

The wilderness is a place of preparation, learning and growth for many. Moses and the Hebrew slaves lived in the wilderness for years, learning much about trusting God and becoming His people before they were able to enter the Promised Land. Centuries later, as they returned from exile in Babylon, they met again with the God who promised that He was "making a way in the wilderness and streams that would flow in the wastelands" (Isaiah 43:19). John the Baptist went to live in the wilderness in preparation for his unique, God-given ministry. Even Jesus, the Son of God, was led into the wilderness to learn who He was and what kind of Messiah He might be.

I'm delighted to say that I no longer have you in my life, ME. God didn't send me into that wilderness but He led me from it and I hope I don't return. But it was a time of discovery and growth, of good coming from bad. I won't ever get those years back and am not the same now as I was then. But God can repay for us the years that the locusts have eaten (Joel 2:25).

Yours delightedly,

Gill

* The official Latin name is Myalgic Encephalomyelitis, which means inflammation of the muscles and brain.

** Pictures of these cards can be found on my website: www.restoredrecycledremade.com

*** From the hymn 'Great is Thy Faithfulness' (Thomas O. Chisholm 1866-1960)

RESTORED RECYCLED REMADE

Maybe there are sometimes a few chinks of light in the darkness of dementia; a few moments of hope in the agony of Alzheimer's.

Chapter 6
Forget-Me-Not

Dear Alzheimer's,

I hate you. I suppose that the word "dear" in the other sense – expensive, costly – is appropriate here because you do cost a lot. For people who have the misfortune to fall into your clutches, the cost is their memories, understanding, abilities, minds and eventually, their lives. You take it from them. Or maybe, it's that you layer other things on top. Rather like the time I decided to give our kitchen a facelift and painted directly onto old paint and varnish, instead of removing it. It looked good but the original surface, the beautiful grain of the wood, could no longer be seen.

Bit by bit, Alzheimer's, you envelop people until the unique, beautiful person is hidden from all; seen only by the Maker Himself. For family and friends, the cost is distress, anger, sadness, helplessness and loss.

If I was feeling generous, I could've said that you also give. You give time: time to make memories, to laugh, to share, to say "Goodbye" (which is possibly better for those left behind than the unforeseen heart attack). In some cases, you teach carers or relatives new things about themselves: patience, love, caring and the ability to see the world through someone else's eyes. But this is by no means a given, and it doesn't begin to make up for your devastating cruelty.

One of the most moving stories in the soap opera 'Emmerdale' was, for me, Ashley's dementia. Ashley, the local vicar who had spent much time caring for others, was diagnosed with dementia and had to let others care for him. He had vascular dementia, not Alzheimer's but a lot of the symptoms were the same. Maybe this was worse to begin with. Ashley knew his diagnosis. He was able to talk to others about it; to reason and face his future. He also knew what was going to happen: that he would, one day, forget his wife, his father and his children. In a TV first, we got to see the world – the fast, confusing, noisy, difficult world – as if through his eyes. It was remarkable.

When Ashley eventually died, it was decided to conclude the story by showing a dream. In this dream Ashley was alive and his old self again and the two of them were able to talk, reminisce and finally say goodbye. During this conversation, Ashley began to apologise for how he upset his wife and the difficulties, heartache and sadness that he had brought upon her. But she interrupted him with the words "and also joy, hope and love."

"I thought I took all those things from you," said Ashley.

"You couldn't take those things from me," whispered Laurel. "Don't ever think that. This last year has been the best year of my life, truly, because I had you."

OK, so that's fiction and possibly a slight case of looking through rose-coloured spectacles because the two of them did have some sticky moments. But I think I get why she said it. For once, Ashley was not rushing around, going to meetings and events and putting everyone else first. And though they may have become increasingly fewer, the tender moments were very tender. Maybe there are sometimes a few chinks of light in the darkness of dementia; a few moments of hope in the agony of Alzheimer's.

But I still hate you. You may give but you take away far more. You have taken, and are taking, some of my family from me.

My great aunt was the first, as far as I'm aware; though I had already heard the word "senile" applied to people who were exhibiting strange behaviour. We hardly ever saw her, so her illness didn't really impact us. I think I was aware that something wasn't quite right. Her letter offering to be a nanny to her "dead sister's children" gave my dad some concern. There were accounts of her putting an electric kettle onto a gas stove and slightly more bizarre tales, such as asking my cousins if they'd ever been introduced to their father. So, something strange was affecting a great aunt who we hardly ever saw. It wasn't something we could do anything about and we were shielded from much of what was going on.

Her son, an only child, was next. Again, we didn't see them that often and I don't think we knew what the problem was to begin with. Dad said he thought his cousin was having a nervous breakdown. He had recently retired and it wasn't certain if the breakdown, if that's what it was, led to the retirement or the retirement caused some kind of breakdown. Even after things deteriorated and there was a diagnosis of Alzheimer's, it was still all rather removed. We didn't see him again and occasionally heard that he was in hospital.

That was the first time that I realised how evil you can be, Alzheimer's. There were occasional bouts of aggression; shouting at nurses and his wife. I'd never heard this gentle, quiet, kindly man raising his voice. How could he now be shouting and throwing things, maybe even to the point of needing restraint? But that's what happens sometimes, isn't it, Alzheimer's: you get into the part of the brain that regulates behaviour and delight in messing it up.

You switched to the other side of the family after that to cause the maximum amount of chaos and afflicted my nan.

Grandma chose to go into sheltered housing a year or two after granddad died and for a while, it was fine. She didn't drive, so travelled round on buses, continued to go bowling and to knit scarves, pullovers and so on for her family and friends. The housing complex was a couple of miles away from us so we saw a fair bit of grandma. Either she came to us – once she had bribed our Alsatian with biscuits – or we dropped in on her.

But, as is the way, she began to become forgetful and, before long, it became clear that she would need more help than the home was able to give. I think that climbing out of her ground floor window in the middle of the night and being found wandering the streets by the police may have been the start.

For a while, my mum and my aunt took it in turns to care for her: a month or two with one daughter then a month or two with the other. I went to visit and help out as often as I could, which wasn't that often. Apart from the forgetfulness and repetition of thoughts and speech, I think one of the biggest concerns was safety, that Grandma shouldn't get out of the house and be able to wander. In her mind, I think she needed to go home in case her mother was wondering where she was.

Though I helped out, I didn't have much to do with Grandma's day to day care, nor with choosing her first care home. I say first, because she was moved at least once, probably as her needs got greater. Until, at last, she was a little old lady occupying a chair in a room; got out of bed in the morning, dressed, sat in the lounge, toileted, fed, watered, toileted, bed. What kind of life is that for an independent, loving, sociable mother, grandmother and great grandmother, prolific knitter, former bowls player and champion? What kind of life is that for anyone? Indeed, is it life at all?

And then, about fifteen years ago, Alzheimer's, you came for my mum. I've sometimes wondered whether illnesses and dementia, in particular, could be triggered by shock. Both my granddad and father died suddenly and unexpectedly: granddad about twenty minutes after the doctor had been there and my dad on the day he was due to be discharged from hospital. Although Grandma and Mum seemed to cope for several months afterwards, could shock have been a catalyst? Could it have weakened the defences somehow so that you could get in, Alzheimer's, and begin to spread your tentacles?

Mum's dementia started in the usual way: repeating the same information on phone and in face to face conversations, asking the same questions and forgetting the answers and forgetting where she'd put things. There were sometimes ingenious explanations for how items came to appear, disappear or get moved around, such as:

"I think someone came into the house while I was in the shower, and took it." Or "My mother must have called in while I was at the shops; she's left me some lunch." As grandma had been dead for several years at that point, we thought it unlikely. That wasn't too bad; far worse was her explanation for why she never saw my dad. "Your father is avoiding me. He leaves the house before I get up and he comes back after I've gone to bed. I think he's having an affair."

Where did that come from? Why did you have to plant that alien idea in her confused, subconscious mind, Alzheimer's? Was it because my father had died before you could get a hold of him, you thought you would sully his memory?

We weren't living too far from Mum then, so I saw more of her and was slightly more involved. Although much of the day to day care and difficult conversations, like telling her she couldn't drive any more, fell upon my brothers. We did what we could. That's what I told myself, anyway. Maybe I should have fought harder. My sister-in-law, who lived streets away, did an amazing job as her carer.

Safety was still a priority. We sometimes arrived at Mum's house to hear stories from the neighbours of how she'd gone into the nearby woods at night looking for her children. I hope those excursions were rare. Usually, she just walked to the local shops, arriving home with the same items that she had bought the day before.

It's a shame that supermarkets are so impersonal. I can't help thinking that if Mum had gone to a little corner shop, a kindly assistant might have told her that she'd bought lots of tinned fruit over the past week and wouldn't she like a nice piece of meat instead? Of course, she might not have been able to cook the nice piece of meat had she bought it, not least because we had turned off the gas. We had to go through a convoluted routine to turn the tap back on when we needed it. If she'd been able to ask such a thing, Mum might well have wondered why the gas only appeared to work when her children were in the house.

Eventually, though, we had to start looking into care homes. We were fortunate, as my oldest brother found one that was close to where he lived. Mum was due to move in on a certain date but, first of all, she decided to have one, final, adventure which involved travelling on as many buses as possible from Petts Wood to Kingston-upon-Thames in one day. That was some journey! She couldn't have known, could she? An observant bus driver saw her and, I think, somehow notified a local hospital. She went into the home the next day.

Of course, there were teething troubles at first. Our story to Mum was that she had to stay there while the roof on her house was being repaired. I'm not sure if she believed us because she was always trying to escape. She once greeted me clutching a pile of clothes and announced that she was going home. As we had, by then, sold our family home that might have been rather difficult. But who knew which home she was referring to? The repairs to her house, mysteriously, went on for a very long time. Until Mum, inevitably, began to settle and accepted that that was where she lived. Occasionally, there was the complaint, though, that her parents hadn't been to see her and so father was probably still in prison (Where did those thoughts come from, Mum?).

And she's still there. In the home, I mean. I think she's probably their longest-staying resident. Other people who we met when Mum first moved in and her partner in crime who helped with the escapades, have long since moved on or died. But Mum is still there. My strong, independent, confident, capable mother is imprisoned; confined to a room in an admittedly lovely care home. My Mum: wife, sister, mother, colleague, friend, sociable hostess, trapped; not by her surroundings, but by her body. Unable to welcome, recognise and provide for family. Unable to speak, to attempt the numbers or conundrum, on 'Countdown' or to tell me, yet again, that I should not carry a black handbag if I'm wearing blue shoes.

Yes, I hate you, Alzheimer's. You impose yourself upon people. You're an unwanted squatter, who gains access to a room, redecorates and settles in and then, gradually, unchallenged, takes over the whole house.

I'm well aware that one day you may try to move in with me too. I will do my best to keep you out – as you have to be the worst housemate ever – but it may not be possible. So I've started to make a memory box, containing a small scrapbook with favourite hymns, Bible readings, poems and my various craft activities, a photo album of Andrew's pictures, and items that are, or have been, important to me. Just so that someone knows, in case the real me should one day get wrapped in your tentacles and hidden.

You won't win, you know. Sadly, it's too late for Mum. But so many people are determined to overcome you now, that I'm certain that this will happen. There are people like my brilliant niece who studied chemistry at university, who are trying to find a way to kill you. Or the thousands of folk who are raising money for research to find drugs that will limit your power, serve you with a restraining order or eviction notice. People who are helping us identify you, to spread the word about what you're like and to let you know that you're not welcome.

You won't win, Alzheimer's; you can't.

Yours defiantly,

Gill

Since writing these words, my lovely Mum has died.

The fight to kill you, goes on.

I hope that you've been remade, restored and that something good has come from something bad.

Chapter 7
Burglar Bill

Dear Burglar (I don't know if your name was Bill),

It was 23 years ago that you, illegally, entered our house and stole from us.

I know this, because I was just out of hospital after an operation on a slipped disc. We were away for the weekend, in Harrogate I think, because I had come joint second in a national poetry competition and I wanted to meet the author who was presenting the prizes. It was a long way to go, the cost of the weekend far exceeded the prize money that I received, and it wasn't that easy getting around on crutches. But I was proud to be a prize winner, so we went.

We came home to find our back gate open, a broken golf club on the lawn and evidence of your presence in our house. It wasn't nice. It cost us money, caused upset and I felt as though I should've hated you. But I never did, in spite of the fact that you took my grandmother's jewellery.

Although I wouldn't condone for one minute what you did, and I wanted my grandmother's jewellery back, it wasn't hard to feel some sympathy for you.

For one thing, you got caught. Thanks for smashing our lightbulbs, by the way. It was that which caused you to cut your hand and leave perfect, or at least clear, finger prints on our window frame as you climbed out again. The fact that you were known to the police also helped. Maybe getting caught was no big deal for you – an occupational hazard, you might say. Maybe there was a part of you that even wanted to be caught. The newspaper article said that you were of no fixed abode and had been high on drugs. Going to prison would've meant that you had a roof over your head for a while, and possibly greater access to drugs than if you'd remained on the outside. When I was a nurse for people with learning disabilities, some of our long term residents were discharged from the hospital because it had been decided – i.e. government policy – that they should live in the community. Some of them soon discovered that the quickest way to get back to the safety of the hospital which they had called "home" all their lives, was to throw a brick through a shop window or steal some small items. Maybe it's the same for those who have been in prison or who are desperate for somewhere to live.

Another reason that I felt sorry for you was because of the jewellery that you took. The police's opinion was that you would've sold it down the pub, so you could have a fix. I can't imagine that you were offered anything close to what it was worth, so somebody even more unscrupulous than you sensed your desperation. Maybe they gave you cash and you were able to buy yourself something to eat. If so, I'm glad. Or maybe they just handed over a little packet of the poison that you so desperately craved. Then you would have been satisfied, for a while. But before too long, you would've had to think about where your next fix was going to come from. You were a prisoner long before you were caught and taken off to jail; trapped in the dependency on your particular choice of drug and the need to think of ways to finance your habit. Talking of drugs, I realised a few days afterwards that you'd taken a bag of tablets that I'd been given on discharge from the hospital. You possibly didn't notice the bed in our living room or wonder why it was there. You probably didn't consider the fact that the medication might have been important for someone. You may have just thanked your lucky stars that you found it. You would have also found out, maybe too late, that some of those tablets were laxatives. I hope it wasn't too unpleasant for you.

All things considered, it's sad that someone should become so dependent on drugs and alcohol that they have to turn to crime. It's sad, really, that any of us may become addicted, or enslaved to anything (whether it's "soft" addictions, such as television, chocolate, shopping, or the more destructive substances like drugs, alcohol or gambling). Even work and sex can become harmful addictions and lead to stress and a breakdown in health or a relationship.

I went to a Christian seminar once, which was called 'Insight into Addictions.' * We learnt that an addiction starts with a sense of loss or deprivation and a need to hide an inner pain. This loss might go back into childhood: the loss of a parent, role model or sibling, maybe. Possibly the loss of confidence, if the person was bullied or belittled; the loss of identity or status if they became unemployed or were made redundant (why is it that our identities are so closely tied up with our work, and we are led to feel that our worth is dependent on what we achieve?). Or the loss might be a recent loss of health or sudden bereavement. This pain can lead to, or trigger, a sense of abandonment or feelings of being unloved, worthless and so on. If this pain is too hard to face or deal with, a person may seek to cover it up or subdue it. This might be by having a drink, going shopping, eating chocolate, burying yourself in work or gambling or some other kind of escapism. As a one-off, that might be fine, but the problem is that it might not stop there. The next time the person thinks of their loss, or experiences the painful emotions, they may reach for the substance which numbed, or distracted them from that pain and gave a few moments of pleasure. This will mean that the next time these feelings occur, they are a little harder to deal with.

Before too long, the person could find that they need a little more of the substance to produce the same pleasant feelings: maybe three drinks instead of two. Whether they realise it or not, they may then be halfway down the slope and heading for addiction. Clearly this is not going to happen to everyone who think, "I need a drink or pick-me-up." But it could.

Neither do I write this with any sense of superiority or judgement. I'm not addicted to chocolate, but I do like it and I recognise that it's still often my "go to" after upsetting or bad news. I've read stories from people who've said the same. They suffered a bereavement and reached for the cake; they were bullied for their weight and turned to food for comfort. I also recognise that there are a number of points in my life when I could have started on the path to addiction. Bereavement, unemployment, illness, disability and other painful life events could have easily caused me to take my first ever drink. Mixing with a different crowd could have led me to start smoking. Frequenting pubs or clubs could have brought me into contact with people who offered me "something to take the edge off." If that had happened and one or more of those things had supplanted chocolate in my affections, I could've well been on the way to becoming an addict. Maybe, for once, my fear of what other people might say served me well.

I said that you were a prisoner long before you were taken off to jail, but the truth is that many, if not all of us, are imprisoned in some way. Maybe we are trapped by our past by painful memories that have a grip on us and won't let go. Maybe we're trapped by thoughtless words, actions or other people's ideas or expectations of us. Maybe we're trapped in grief, either an actual bereavement, which seems impossible to recover from, or the loss of a job, or hopes and dreams. And who can say how any of us will deal with that loss or sense of deprivation?

Anyway, back to you, Mr Burglar.

I don't know who you are, where you are or what you're doing. You may be on your ninth prison sentence. Or maybe our break-in was your last, you went to rehab in prison and turned your life around. You may have watched the Jesus of Nazareth video that, bizarrely, you also stole from us and you could've become a Christian in the meantime. There are a number of people who can testify to God's amazing love; a love which reaches down, even to a prison cell. It's a love which can release captives, cleanse, forgive and renew. Joseph, whose story you can read later in this section, realised that God was with him in his prison cell. If you did find God, or rather if God found you, while you were in prison and if you have experienced his life-changing love, then I'm glad.

That's not to say that what you did wasn't a big deal and I'm not trying to excuse, or dismiss, your behaviour. You had no right to enter, destroy and remove our property. As you were known to the police, this wasn't your first crime. Who knows how many other people you robbed, violated or even physically hurt along the way? You could've turned over a new leaf by now and be a new creation in God's eyes – but you still did those things. Whether or not your victims, for want of a better word, have been able to forgive you is not for me to say. I hope that they have, at least, been able to find comfort, healing and peace within themselves.

You may be dead, Mr Burglar and if you are, then I'm sorry. Sorry because, although I never got my jewellery back, I still have memories. I still have memories of my grandmother wearing the engagement ring she was given when she was twenty one. I still have memories of her telling us about her father in the Royal Scots Fusiliers, who had a fob watch with a very long chain and had a section of that chain cut in half and made into bracelets for his two daughters. That bracelet was quite valuable, being made from rose gold. I won't get it back but the memories are priceless and I still have those.

What memories do you have, Mr Burglar? Maybe you have memories of going to court and seeing the disappointment and hurt that you'd caused to others. Or maybe you only have memories of the inconvenience of being caught and taken away to be locked up.

If you're dead, what memories did you leave for others? What would they have said about you in your eulogy? Do you have children who grew up learning that their dad was always "away?" Or memories that you were never at their sport days or parents evenings; never there to give a word of congratulation, advice or correction? Did they get in with the wrong crowd and go off the rails themselves, because they didn't have a good role model? Were they afraid that they were destined to be like you when they grew up? Did you have a wife who had long since discovered that you weren't the man she married and who looked for comfort and support elsewhere? Did, or does, your family try to gloss over your existence and airbrush your name from the family tree? Did you live your whole life without discovering who you were and who you were made to be?

Or are you still alive and have struggled to come off drugs and put your criminal past behind you? Have you, somehow, tried to make amends for your crimes? Are you able to talk to and help others who were trapped, as you once were? Have you made, or can you make, a positive contribution to society? Have you met the God who can make all things new?

I can't remember if the idea of criminals meeting with the victims of their crime was around twenty-three years ago; maybe not. Or maybe it was but we weren't offered the opportunity. I may not have been able to tell you all of this at the time but I hope I'd have tried to explain and to ask why you did it. Maybe you committed later crimes and other people had that opportunity. Maybe this gave you a short, sharp shock and you finally have some idea of what you put others through.

I don't know.

But I do hope that you are no longer imprisoned by a dependency on drugs or a life of crime. You weren't made for that kind of life. I hope that you've been remade, restored and that something good has come from something bad. I hope that you've been able to make amends, find peace and are able to help others do the same. Then, what happened to us wouldn't have been in vain.

Yours hopefully,

Gill

* A CWR course, at Waverly Abbey, Farnham Surrey

Further details on the Resources Page.

RESTORED RECYCLED REMADE

God can take the worst, most difficult situations and use them for good or bring good from them.

Chapter 8
Joseph's story

My name is Joseph, and I'm only too happy to tell you the story of how God worked in my messy life and brought something new out of it.

I grew up in a family with eleven brothers; yes, eleven!

The story of how that came about will have to wait for another day but suffice it to say that Dad had two wives at the same time and most of my brothers had different mothers. My mum was the love of my dad's life and she had also, for a long time, been unable to give him children. Then I was born. Some years after that she gave birth to my brother Benjamin which, sadly, cost her life. I'm afraid that I was rather spoilt as a child, probably for that reason, while, for a few years, Dad found it quite hard to look at Ben. My other brothers didn't bother with me much. It must've been hard knowing that Dad didn't love their mother.

I remember that Dad once gave me a lovely, multicoloured coat, which I just loved to wear. The others said that I did it to show off. But when I wore it I remembered, and knew, how much Dad loved me. It made me feel safe.

Apart from being part of a huge and rather dysfunctional family, I had an unremarkable childhood. Only two things stood out really: a couple of dreams that I had. In the first, my brothers and I were in a field, gathering corn and binding it into sheaves. Suddenly, my sheaf of corn stood upright and their sheaves gathered round it and bowed down to it. Figuring I might have been eating too much cheese before bedtime, I said nothing to anyone for some time. But then I told my brothers about it. Most of them are way older and, I dare say, wiser than I am. I wasn't boasting. I wanted to know what they thought it meant and whether it was a sign for my future. But I suppose that, coming so soon after the multicoloured coat, it might have seemed like I was showing off, again. The boys were scornful: "What? Are you going to try to rule over us?"

But then I had another dream. In this one the sun, moon and even the stars were bowing down to me. Maybe these dreams were meant to reassure me in some way. I was nearly the youngest in a large family, I could have easily been overlooked and lost in the crowd. But why did Benjamin not have any such dreams?

Was I going to be a leader? It seemed so, after having almost the same dream twice. Did God send these dreams? If so, what was He saying? What did He want?

I didn't know, but I asked the boys again anyway. Maybe they would realise, with the dream being almost repeated, that it meant something. Well, that was a mistake. If they hadn't been jealous of me before that, they certainly were afterwards. Even Dad was critical.

One day, Dad said he wanted me to go to a field where my brothers were working and see how they were getting on. It took me a while to track them down. But they saw me before I saw them and, unknown to me, started plotting to get rid of "that dreamer." This apparently involved dipping my coat in the blood of an animal and then lying to our father that I had been mauled to death. It seems that Reuben, the oldest, stood up for me and argued that I should be thrown into an empty well instead. He, I think, had secret plans to rescue me.

Well, he got his way, and I was left shivering at the bottom of a cistern in the middle of the wilderness. I don't want to think about what might have happened next. But, in fact, the boys were hungry by this time, sat down for a meal, noticed a group of Ishmaelites on their way to Egypt and hit on a change of plan. Judah (I've always liked him) persuaded the others that covering up a murder would not end well. So, why not make some money by selling me into slavery? This sounded good, so they hauled me out of the cistern and I was sold for twenty pieces of silver. They went ahead with the rest of their plan though – Dad must have been devastated.

Once in Egypt, the Ishmaelites decided to sell me on to someone else: Potiphar, one of Pharaoh's officials, no less. I do hope they got more than twenty pieces of silver for me; I think I'm worth more than that.

There's nothing like being in a foreign country to make you realise that you miss home, and the traditions and practices of home suddenly become very important.

I had heard Dad talking about the God of his fathers and how He had spoken to and led them. Apart from possibly sending me those two dreams, though, this God hadn't really been that important to me. Yet, it seemed that He was with me now in Egypt. Everything that I did was suddenly good and bore fruit. Even my master noticed that God seemed to be favouring me, so he made me his attendant. That may have been more in the hope that some of this divine favour would rub off on him too. But no matter; I was put in charge of Potiphar's entire household – everything that he owned. This was much better than a dusty cistern in the wilderness. Dad's God had come through for me.

Why, then, did I suddenly find myself in prison?

It seemed that my master's wife had decided that I should perform a special, personal, duty for her, to put it politely. I refused and soon discovered the meaning of the phrase "a woman scorned." Before I knew it, I was being accused of molestation, or worse. I might have been head of his household but I was still, basically, a slave. I couldn't defend myself and there was no chance that the master would listen to me over his wife.

So there I was, unfairly accused and thrown into prison, uncertain about my fate. There was no guarantee that, this time, I would be rescued.

Where was God now in this roller-coaster of my life?

Why had He given me dreams which had hinted at so much and then taken them away again? I didn't sleep with my master's wife, not because of her but because it would have been a sin against God. So why had He done this to me? I soon discovered, though, that God hadn't left me alone in that jail, but He was there with me. I began to believe and to really know that for myself. And before too long, it seemed others came to see it as well. The warder trusted me to take charge of everything that was going on. So much so that he left me to it. He was content that if I took something on or said I would do something, it would be done.

One day, we had two new arrivals; nothing unusual in that except that these were two of Pharaoh's employees: his chief cupbearer and chief baker. Goodness knows what they had done to deserve such displeasure. Maybe they had ordered the wrong wine or put too many candles on Pharaoh's cake?

Anyway, as was now becoming customary, they were assigned to me. One morning I could see that they were each preoccupied with something. It turned out that each had had a dream and there was no one to interpret what these dreams meant. Now, I knew something about dreams. True, it seemed as though I was not seeing mine fulfilled. But I knew by now that it was God who had given me my dreams and it was only He who could give the interpretation. So, I asked them to tell me about them and then I prayed. The cupbearer's dream had a favourable meaning: within three days he was going to be restored to his former position. I couldn't help adding that, maybe, when he was restored, he might put in a good word for me. I didn't think that was unreasonable. The meaning of the chief baker's dream was, sadly, not so good. There was to be no forgiveness for this man and he would be executed within three days.

Three days later, the cupbearer was restored to his former position. But he forgot about my request and I was left in that place for a further two years. It might have been even longer but Pharaoh had a couple of dreams of his own one night, which involved cows.

Seven of the cows were fat and they were eaten by seven other cows who were skinny. Pharaoh had no idea what the dreams meant. He asked everyone and, eventually, his cupbearer reminded him of me. I was sent for, appeared before Pharaoh and was able to give him the news that the land would soon become very prosperous for seven years. There was nothing to be complacent about, however, because those bountiful years were to be followed by seven years of famine. I advised him that the wisest thing to do would be to store grain and food during the years of prosperity so that they'd be able to survive those lean years.

That was that, as far as I was concerned: Pharaoh had a dream and God told me what the meaning was. If I'd thought about it, I might have been tempted to plead my cause to Pharaoh, who would surely have been favourable towards me after that. But, in fact, I didn't get a chance. Pharaoh declared that I was the only one who could oversee this project and the practicalities of storing, and much later, distributing the food. Such an honoured, yet daunting task. I'd never have said that I was capable of it. But years of managing Potiphar's household, plus several more attending to prisoners, had taught me some skills that I might otherwise not have had. I also had the greatest assurance of all: that God was with me. Maybe I even had to go through those other things to learn to know and trust Him.

Anyway, that's what happened. I was set free, given a cloak and a gold chain and was pronounced to be second in command. People came to me for help, advice and food.

I recognised them as soon as they sidled into my presence: ten men older, slightly gaunt, asking for something to eat. My brothers! I'd occasionally wondered what I might do if I ever saw them again. They didn't know about anything that had happened to me since I'd been in Egypt, yet their actions had sent me here in the first place. Prior to that, they'd planned to kill me.

Maybe there was a moment when I wanted to remind them of my childhood dreams and that they were now bowing at my feet. Maybe there was a momentary flashback to being in that cistern: me hungry while they feasted. Now they were hungry and I had the power to withhold food from them. But I'd changed and, suddenly, I was desperate to know if they had, too.

I pretended that I thought that they were spies and was rather stern with them. This spooked them and they began talking amongst themselves – not realising that I understood every word. I then appeared to reconsider and asked them to tell me about the family. They said that Dad was still alive! I don't know how I didn't lose it there and then.

I won't bore you with details but, after giving them the grain they wanted, I engineered the situation so that Benjamin appeared to have stolen a valuable cup from me. When I "discovered" this, I complained that he'd abused my hospitality and demanded that he be thrown into jail.

Then Judah stepped forward (just as he had stood up for me all those years before) and offered to go to jail in Ben's place. It seems that Dad had been very reluctant to let his youngest travel to Egypt. He'd only agreed after Judah had promised to take care of him and personally guaranteed his safety. The lads feared for Dad's health if they were to return without Benjamin, the only remaining son, they thought, of Dad's beloved wife.

After that, I had no choice. "I am Joseph," I told them; though I was crying so much I could scarcely get the words out. My brothers were shocked and rather frightened too. Maybe they had told themselves that I really had died. Maybe they believed I was going to punish them. I, their wronged brother, now held all the power.

Then I remembered my dreams. I remembered, too, my messy life: all I'd been through over the years. God hadn't planned for me to be sold as a slave, falsely accused and thrown into jail. But He had been with me in all of that and had brought me to this place. I was now a leader; the dreams had been fulfilled.

I told the lads that they were not to be distressed and to blame themselves for what had happened and that what "they had meant for evil, God meant it for good."

Unsurprisingly, it took a while for them to understand, accept or even believe what I was telling them. But we were together again and they brought Dad to Egypt.

Some years later, Dad died. I was glad to have found him again and glad that he knew that I had met, and knew, the God of our fathers. Dad was even able to meet my children.

His death saddened, but didn't hurt me. What hurt was that my brothers were scared that I might now take revenge on them for all those lost years. So, they told me that it had been Dad's final wish that I should forgive them.

Oh boys! Didn't you know that it was God who had given me those childhood dreams of leadership? Didn't you know that it was God who had sent me to Egypt, ahead of you, to save lives? Don't you understand that it was God who had kept me safe through the rough times and put me in that position of power and leadership? Since God was in control and knew what He was doing, why would I have wanted to punish you?

They didn't get it.

God can take the worst, most difficult situations and use them for good or bring good from them. It's not luck or coincidence that beautiful things can come from something bad. Even if the painful situation is of our making or doing, God can recreate and make all things -- and people – new.

GILL TAGGART

Remade

God wants us to know that we can be His children, His witnesses and ambassadors.

Chapter 9
In Search of God's Will

Dear God's Will,

I'm afraid I don't really know who you are.

I've been trying to discover your identity for many years. It seems that I'm not the only one. I've often heard people asking, "Is this God's Will?" I've been told, "God has a plan for your life; you must find out if this is God's Will for you." Or "You shouldn't miss God's Will for you."

Well, here's the thing: if God had a specific, tailored, detailed plan for my life, why wouldn't He tell me what it is? Why wouldn't He tell any of us? In fact, why not hand us a plan or logbook when we become Christians?

"In September 1980, you will apply for and be given job X. You are to work hard for two years and then apply for promotion, which you will get. After four further years, you will be asked to apply for Job Y; another promotion. You must turn this down and answer a call to ordained ministry. You will be ordained and do many different things; help people, set up a charity, preach in front of famous people and then you can retire."

Or "You will become a nurse/teacher/judge/police officer/plumber which you will do for many years in hospitals, schools courtrooms or offices, all over the country."

I know God doesn't want robots. He has chosen to let us choose for ourselves, so He is not going to dictate our lives, or hand us a pre-written script for them.

But, God's Will, you are still something that nearly all Christians say that I have to look for, seek and discover. So, could you try not to be so elusive please?

Some Christians who claim to have found, defined and nailed you down give out mixed messages about you – even, occasionally, those in leadership.

"You have a passion for pastoral work? How do you know that they are not your own desires, rather than God's Will?"

"What do you want to do; what is your God-given passion?"

"You don't want to do missionary work? Are you willing to do God's will instead of pleasing yourself?"

"What kind of jobs are you drawn to? What do you want to do?"

"It doesn't matter if you don't think you can do that; when God calls, He always provides."

"If you haven't been given those gifts, why would God call you to do that? Why would you even apply for it?"

I have encountered, debated, questioned and tried to understand all of this.

Years ago, I had a very brief spell at teacher's training college. I didn't want to go. If my experiences of Sunday school were anything to go by, teaching was not for me. But I didn't know what else to do, so I went.

In our second term, we started teaching practice: one day a week in a school. It didn't take me long – about six hours I think – to discover that my previous instincts had been correct: I was in the wrong place. Back at college, other students were buzzing, talking excitedly about being in a real classroom and taking the first steps in their new careers. I said nothing, and my friends sensed that I wanted to be alone. I told myself that it would get better once I started actually teaching and got some confidence.

It didn't.

I tried to persuade myself not to give up at the first hurdle. Christians also tried to encourage me: "You know, if it wasn't God's will for you to be here, you wouldn't be." "Sometimes His will is hard, but you have to persevere." "It will get easier, but if you give up now you'll never know. And you'll miss out on the job that God wants for you."

None of that really helped.

The best advice came from my tutors, who said, "One day a week in school is not realistic; wait until your five-week block teaching practice in the second year." That did it; there was no way I was going into a classroom every day for five weeks. Decision made.

My gut feeling, or instinct, had told me before I even went to college that teaching was not for me. But I hadn't followed it because, apparently, God's Will was contrary to my own thoughts, desires and ideas.

I had wanted, from about the age of eighteen or nineteen, to do pastoral work in or for the church. More than that, I somehow knew that this was what I would be doing with my life. I just didn't know if it was to be full-time, part-time, paid, voluntary or if I was meant to have a career in something else as well.

Several years after this, I began to wonder if God was calling me to join the Church Army, which I always describe as the Church of England's equivalent of the Salvation Army. I dismissed it to begin with. That wasn't pastoral work. I would be trained as an officer in evangelism. I didn't do evangelism. It made me think of Billy Graham and my gifts weren't in that area. But if God was calling, then He was calling and saying, "No, I don't fancy it," wasn't an option. Besides, I soon learned that the Church Army commissioned officers to work in parishes, prisons, hostels and care homes. Officers in these settings were involved in a number of activities which weren't, overtly, evangelistic. So maybe I was wrong and there were different kinds of evangelism.

I decided to test it out rather than plunge in headfirst, so I applied to join the Church Army's Christian Service Scheme (CSS). This involved being sent to different placements for up to a year to see something of the work of Church Army and to work with, or alongside, officers. There were a lot of applicants for this and only a few places. But to my surprise, I was accepted. The overseer of the CSS later told me that she knew she was going to accept me as I had so much to offer. Well, that was nice.

My first placement was in a hostel for homeless women in Marylebone, North London. Towards the end of this time, I felt that I was still being called to join the Church Army. I had seen nothing to put me off or to make me feel that it was wrong for me. So, I applied. I was asked to go for an interview, which I passed and then was invited to a selection weekend. Christian friends told me that they thought the Church Army was right for me and that I'd do well. The warden of the hostel said that he wouldn't offer me the full-time job that was coming up because I would be going to college. The Church Army officer who was then overseeing the CSS didn't even find me a second placement because I wouldn't need it. I had talked, prayed, thought about this and felt that I had done what I could to discern God's Will. It seemed to be confirmed by others, even a Church Army officer.

Yet, I wasn't accepted for training.

I must admit that it wasn't too disappointing because the Church Army, which doesn't normally tell people why they were being turned down, told me it was because I had pastoral gifts rather than evangelistic ones. The recommendation was that I think about becoming a deaconess in the Church of England. Which was what I had wanted to do in the first place!

(That didn't work out either, though.)

After a stint as a care worker for people with learning disabilities, I applied and was accepted to train as a nurse. "Great," I thought, "I've discovered God's Will at last." Three years later, I was diagnosed with ME and left before my final exams.

Around twenty years after this, when I was emerging from my wilderness years with ME and just finishing my preacher's training, I believed it might be God's Will for me to be ordained as a Methodist Minister. Again, I thought, discussed, prayed, read and searched – all the things you're supposed to do as a Christian. Again, the assurances came: "You'll be a great Minister, Gill. You're so good with people!" And not just once, but half a dozen times. Long story short, several attempts came to nothing.

So what did all of that mean? Even now, it's hard to make sense of it all. Was it God's Will for me to be a teacher, Church Army Officer, Deaconess, Nurse, Methodist Minister or any of the other things I tried to explore? Apparently not!

Was I so deaf to God and so stubbornly determined to go my own way that the only way I could be stopped was by failure? Was it God's Will for me to go through all of this, just to try to find God's Will?

There are certainly people who seem to think that God's Will is anything that happens to us. Are you in a dead-end job? It's God's Will. Unemployed? God's Will! Single, married, unhappily married, rich, poor, sick, disabled? God's Will! Maybe they find some comfort in that belief. I can even understand why they may hold it, though, to me, it sounds fatalistic, even lazy. But taken to its logical conclusion, that means that every tragic, evil thing that has ever happened – wars, the holocaust, rapes, killings, accidents caused by drunk drivers, abusive spouses, terrorist attacks and so on – are all God's Will. And I don't accept that for one moment.

I don't accept that God, who is love, plans evil. It's humans who are greedy, who go to war, drop bombs, cheat, lie, injure or kill others. Some decide to get behind the wheel of a car after they've been drinking. A few who are irritated/depressed by life, their job or their marriage and don't have the energy to go to the gym, use their spouse as a punch bag instead.

If none of these bad things are God's Will, then why does He allow them and why doesn't He do anything to stop them? I'm not sure that there's a single answer and certainly not an easy one. But one reason is that God allows us to make our own choices. We're not puppets or conditioned to behave only in a certain way; to believe in God and do as He tells us without question. God has given us certain guidelines for our benefit, not His. He doesn't force us to keep them. It breaks His heart to see us go our own way, yet no matter how He feels and whatever the cost to Himself, He allow us to do so. After being given the freedom to reject God's guidelines and God Himself, and do our own thing, however, isn't it a bit unrealistic to expect God to prevent or change the results of our actions?

"Why don't you do anything about this, God?"

Could it be that God is asking us the same question?

So, if God allows us to make our own choices, was I making the wrong choices for much of my life and He needed to stop me? Maybe or maybe I was correct when I felt that something was wrong for my life. Should I've listened to my instincts and did I experience problems and failures because I didn't listen? Maybe I shouldn't have listened to encouragement from other Christians or words from the pulpit which challenged me to take risks for God and step out in faith. Maybe I should have tried harder to find you, God's Will; prayed harder, asked more people. Maybe it was God's Will that I did what I did. Maybe it wasn't.

Before I go completely mad – though some would say it's too late for that – a question: Do you, God's Will, actually exist?

I can hear the protests from here: "Of course there is such a thing as God's Will. Don't you know there is a verse which says, 'I know the plans I have for you; plans to give you a future and a hope'?"

Yes, I do. But that verse isn't about our futures and doesn't say that God's Will is defined by a particular career. God doesn't teach that His will is only one thing and that we can thwart His will by going to the "wrong" school, university or church. Nor that we will be in trouble if we're unable to find His will for our lives.

A few years ago, I discovered something very interesting. There **are** several verses in the New Testament which teach about God's Will and they're all about being, rather than doing.

Jesus said that it is God's will that everyone who accepts Him should have eternal life, John 6:40. Paul said that it's God's will that we should be holy (1 Thessalonians 4:3). He also said that it's God's will that we rejoice always, pray at all times and give thanks in all circumstances (1 Thessalonians 5:16-18).

Believe in Jesus, rejoice and live holy, prayerful, thankful lives. This is God's will.

God created us. We've been made in His image, He loves us and He wants us to know that. He wants us to believe in, and accept, Jesus. He wants us to be forgiven, to receive fulness of life and every spiritual blessing that there is: joy, peace, security, assurance, hope and more. God wants us to know that we can be His children, His witnesses and ambassadors; salt and light in this dark world. And that we can become the people that we were made to be.

I really don't think that God minds if we do this as a priest or a plumber, a chaplain or a chef, an evangelist or an electrician. I'm not sure that He loses sleep over someone who is living their best life and serving Him as a shop assistant when they "should" be a teacher. Or that He is going to be angry with someone who is a hairdresser when He wanted them to be a nurse. He might be disappointed if we opt for second best: if someone settles for being a shopkeeper when they have the potential to be a teacher. Or if we don't use the gifts He's given us and settle for mediocrity, instead of living the fullness of life that Jesus came to give. He might be disappointed if a person was in a good, worthy, God-given job yet was not living a holy, thankful, prayerful, joyful life. If someone is in the "right place" but isn't growing in faith and love, using their God-given gifts and showing Godly qualities, are they doing God's will? Are they living as the people God made them to be?

Do you exist, God's Will?

Absolutely – but maybe not as we know it.

Best wishes, Gill.

To anyone who has ever been hurt by the church, I'm sorry.

Chapter 10
Church

To the Church,

I once heard someone say that if we're going to criticise or say something negative to someone, we should first say something positive. So with that in mind, I certainly don't hate you.

People have different faiths, or none, different beliefs and values, different ideas about how to find restoration and healing...that's fine.

But I believe that Jesus makes all things new and the church (I hope) preaches Jesus: the man who was also God, who healed the sick and unclean, ate with tax collectors and sinners and valued the poor; the man who lived a spotless life, then offered that life as a sacrifice for the sins of mankind. The church preaches the One who sets the prisoners free, offers forgiveness, cleansing, the washing away of sins and stains and who gives people a new start; the One in whom all things are made new. Stories abound of people who gave up drugs, alcohol, a life of crime, gambling or some other addiction and those who were rescued from loveless, violent, controlling environments, from cults, from despair or from prison, because they met and put their faith in Jesus, who gave them new hope new purpose and new life.

The Church has restored, does restore and can be instrumental in restoring people.

I have certainly been helped, taught, comforted, challenged and changed by the ministry of the Church, which consists of Christian believers incidentally and not the dilapidated building at the end of the road. I've belonged to Bible study groups, youth clubs, social groups, sung in the choir, played in music groups, helped with Brownies, Sunday school and much more. I've heard some great and inspirational sermons and met countless lovely, challenging, friendly, prayerful people who I may never have otherwise met and who've all touched my life in one way or another.

I've been to different churches, learnt new ways of worship, taken on new responsibilities, new experiences and been encouraged to push myself further than I thought possible. I've met lots of people: young, old, disabled and from many cultures. It's amazing that generous, committed, faithful loving people with whom I get on well, people I might otherwise cross the road to avoid, even people in other countries whom I will never, ever meet, are all part of God's family. Even if we have nothing at all in common and don't even speak the same language, we have the same faith, believe the same Gospel, have the same heavenly Father and, for that reason, are inextricably linked as Christian brothers and sisters.

Christian fellowship and worship in the Church does much to restore us, encourage us in our faith and introduce others to the God who restores and heals.

But I'm afraid that, to borrow a well-known phrase, I also have some things against you. You may find it appropriate that there are three points, all beginning with the same letter.

Firstly, **Denominations.**

I hate denominations, always have. As a teenager or young adult, I decided that I was going to belong to as many different denominations as possible, preferably at the same time, so that no one could label me and I could just be a Christian. I get that we're all different, that we all have different ways of worshipping and of reading and applying Scripture. And some may value certain practices, teachings or doctrines above others. But this should not be a cause for division. We're all believers. We have the same God, the same Gospel, the same Saviour, the same Spirit. We all have the same commandment: to love as Jesus loved. We all have the same mission: to make disciples. We're all children of God and heirs with Christ.

Yet, we treat one another appallingly. I've been denied communion by one section of the Church because I'm not "one of them." I'm sure they'd see it differently, but that's how it felt to me. I've been told that my preacher's training is "not valid" in one denomination and that I need to train again. Similarly, practices in one denomination may be frowned upon or not recognised by another one.

And as for working together, it took years of debates, arguments and probably hurt and disappointment for the Anglicans to agree to a covenant with the Methodist church. My family were Anglicans but some of us belonged to, or led, uniformed organisations in the local Methodist Church. The two local churches got on well. Yet when a formal covenant was proposed between the two denominations, it was rejected. I remember my mum apologising to the Methodist Minister for that decision; disappointed that her church didn't want to be in unity with his. Then there was the Christmas card incident.

Many years ago, a Christmas card was being sent around our local churches to be signed and passed on. Each church added their greetings, except one, which refused to sign because a certain denomination had already done so. Whatever the reasons behind that decision, they were not willing to offer Christmas greetings to other churches. That wasn't the best sign of Christian unity. As far as I can see, having different denominations causes more problems than it solves.

Secondly, **Divisive practices**.

Divisive practices probably occur because we have so many denominations.

We practice different things, have different gifts and do things in different ways. Variety is good; we don't all have to be robots. The small differences aren't really too important. Wear robes, use incense, tithe, dance in the aisles or don't – it's all good!

But it's not all good when holy sacraments become a source of division and lead to exclusion. We argue about baptism: Should we do it? How deep should the water be? At what age should people be baptised? About confirmation: is it necessary, or Biblical? Can a person receive communion without it? Why or why not?

Some Christians take communion in one church, change denominations and have to be confirmed before they are allowed to receive it in their new church. At what age should someone be confirmed? Two of my nephews were baptised in the Greek Orthodox church and confirmed at the same time. Some people aren't confirmed until much later. Some people take communion from an early age, others aren't allowed to take it before confirmation. My grandfather was confirmed twice: once at the age of fourteen and again with everyone else in the Royal Navy. A friend became a Christian at university and received communion and continued to receive it for two years at our church before someone realised he hadn't been confirmed. Yet neither of these people were struck down or stunted in their spiritual growth.

We argue, too, about Holy Communion, or the Lord's Supper. Should we have wafers or real bread? Wine or fruit juice? Chalice or individual cups? What age should someone be before we invite them to the Lord's table? Who should lead the communion service? On occasion, churches have missed out on communion due to a shortage of clergy and because no one else is allowed to lead it. Why not? Does God really mind?

What is "communion" anyway? If we're constantly in communion, or fellowship, with God, isn't taking bread and wine on our own, or in a group, just as much "communion" as taking a small wafer that has been blessed by a member of the clergy? Why does it need to be an ordained Minister? What's the difference between a vicar asking for God's blessing upon bread and wine and a child asking for God's blessing on a meal? The New Testament tells us that believers broke bread daily, not that they had a service with one person presiding. Paul criticised the Corinthians for their behaviour at the Lord's Supper and not because they used the wrong kind of bread, or because some were too young to understand or because they didn't wait for an Apostle to come and lead them.

No doubt someone will tell me that I'm naïve or that I have bad theology or I'm too simplistic. But the Gospel is simple – it's we who overcomplicate it. Christians should believe, be baptised and filled with His Spirit, follow Jesus, live out their faith and have regular fellowship with Him and with others. These things are of prime importance. Not much else is.

It's also not good when buildings, furniture or practices hinder unity or become gods. I've heard suggestions that small churches join together to form one larger church; which seems obvious to me, given the shortage of resources. Or that two denominations join together, which, apart from anything else, would give a good Christian witness to the area. But such suggestions are met with horror by some at the thought of surrendering "their" building/pulpit/organ/traditions. "If they want to join with us, fine, but we're not moving or giving that up." So, a community might boast four or five churches, each with a few dozen people which are all struggling, instead of having one larger, united church with four times the number of resources, providing a greater witness. I know Christians who no longer go to church on a Sunday because of these and other arguments. They still believe, read Scripture and meet with other Christians; in fact, they might say that their faith is stronger now. But they've been too hurt by arguments over church practice to want to stay.

If people will know, and recognise, that we belong to Jesus because of our love for others, what will they think of our divisions and arguments?

And thirdly, **Disappointing Worship**.

Now before I get driven out of town, let me say that there are doubtless many churches that have a large membership and lively worship with all ages contributing. This may also be happening in much smaller churches, where two or three are gathered, and so on. And I am not for one minute saying that worship is insincere. The disappointment for me is the nature of the services.

I can't help thinking that a church service should be a means to an end. We should meet together to worship God and hear his Word, pray for and with one another, encourage one another and share testimonies of what God is doing, so that we are strengthened, encouraged and equipped to go out and be salt and light in the world in the following week.

Very often, though, it seems as though the service is the end product: the focus of the organising, rota planning and flower arranging. Worship itself is led by just a few people or maybe even only one. There may be opportunities for members of the congregation to do Bible readings and in some churches they may lead prayers, too. Some churches may have worship leaders, a worship group, a choir or drama team, which is fantastic. But there doesn't seem to be too many of those.

I'm not sure that the concept of believers gathering together and relying on one person, or a couple of people, for their worship is a New Testament one. In his letter to the Corinthians, Paul talks of believers coming together and each having something to contribute to the time of fellowship and worship. That wouldn't be impossible, would it? Surely Christians, who have been faithfully attending church each week, know something of the Bible and have a favourite, or puzzling, passage they could bring to be discussed? Or a favourite, or meaningful hymn that could be sung? Surely, someone would've seen God working in their life during the previous week; been asked a challenging question, received an answer to prayer or tried to put the sermon into practice?

Maybe people could be encouraged to look for God at work in their lives and the world so that they had something to contribute the following week? If this didn't happen at all, then maybe that would be a subject for discussion: "Does what you hear on a Sunday make any difference to you on a Monday?" If people weren't willing to talk about their own faith or journey with God, maybe they support a Christian charity or sponsor children and could bring news of these? Maybe church services could be more like our Bible study groups, which are often encouraging times of real fellowship and learning. If they were, maybe there wouldn't be the mild panic that seems to arise if a church has no one to do the service that week. I have sometimes been met with a feeling of relief if I've "rescued" a church which had no preacher; their service could now go ahead. But couldn't it have done so anyway?

Maybe we shouldn't have services at all and just gather to read Scripture, pray and be with God. Maybe we shouldn't even have church buildings. A century or so ago, everybody went to church, either because there was nothing else to do or because it was expected. Buildings were erected "to the glory of God" and I have no doubt that the builders were sincere about that. A church-going population needed church buildings.

Times have changed.

Today, people aren't often to be found in church on Sundays but in pubs, supermarkets, cafés, beside the canal or in sports halls. So why not rent pubs, libraries, cinemas or coffee bars for our fellowship gatherings, instead of owning and using all our resources to maintain buildings? Buildings can be used for mission, for giving shelter to the homeless, for feeding the hungry. But they also require a lot of time, money and the people willing to look after them.

Why not spend that time and money on a Gospel double decker bus, camper van or boat? Today – even if they believe that faith is relevant to their lives – people don't need to come into a church building to read the Bible or hear a sermon. Worship songs, sermons and the Bible are available on the internet, radio or television; they can be watched or listened to, recorded and downloaded. Worship is and should be far more than a hymn/prayer sandwich on Sunday morning.

So, the church, in my view, also needs to be restored and do some things in a new way. We offer hope and healing to others but we also need to seek that for ourselves; we're not perfect.

To anyone who has ever been hurt by the church, I'm sorry. We don't always get it right. We may be carried away by zeal or stuck in the rut of tradition. However, I still hope that we may be able to introduce you to Jesus, the One who makes all things new and who can help you to become the person you were made to be.

Yours, in faith and hope,
Gill

We can't always see someone else's scars, and our words or actions might be the barb that causes the wound to reopen.

Chapter 11
Dear Reader

Dear Reader,

The idea for this book came after I found myself with a lot of destructive thoughts, past hurts and unresolved incidents buzzing around in my head like demented wasps. Rather than keep them in my head, I decided to write down what I wanted to say and to write to someone how I'd been hurt over the years and what has happened since. The child in me was keen to say, "You said this about me, but just look at what I'm doing now." It's basically a grown up way of saying, "I told you so."

Of course, I never intended to show any of these scribblings to anyone else, never mind having them published. Among other things, I didn't want to be done for libel!

But then I found myself writing about abstract concepts and things that had angered or hurt, me – such as illness, bereavement or disability – and how I came, or was helped, through those times. It occurred to me, then, that others may have been hurt by the same things, words or attitudes and that it might be good to offer words of hope and healing instead of words of anger or accusation.

I started this book by writing about damaged furniture. Sometimes I've tried my hand at a little upcycling or restoration "as they do on the telly." More often than not, I've lacked the patience and the correct tools to do the job properly and ended up painting over cracks, stains or dents. This might look good initially, but it's just cosmetic. Sometimes, layers of paint and stained varnish need to be removed to expose the beautiful wood underneath.

Cracks don't always have to be disguised or papered over. You may have heard the story of a man who was carrying two jars of water. One of the jars was cracked and, as he walked along, water began trickling out. When he reached home, there was only a little water left in the jar. The jar that was full was rather proud of itself and scornful of the second jar for not being able to do its job properly. But the man turned round and pointed out all the beautiful flowers that were growing on one side of the road; the side that had been watered by the leaky jar.

Someone once said to me the more cracked you are, the more people will see the light of Jesus shining through. Cracks or scars are part of who we are and may not need to be hidden. They may spur us on to make change in our lives or the world, or lead to greater empathy with others.

But a scar still hurts if it's unhealed. Unhealed scars may lead to infection and too many unhealed scars in a life might lead to brokenness..

If we feel that we've been badly hurt, that our life has gone downhill thanks to someone else's comments or interference; that our career has ended due to illness, or whatever else – there are a number of ways we can try to mend what is broken; to restore or repurpose the bits that have gone bad. As I was preparing to write this book, I was introduced to the Japanese art of Kintsugi. This word means "golden repairs" and is the art of mending broken items using glue mixed with gold. It's said that a Japanese emperor once broke a valuable item and sent it to be repaired. When it was sent back, the repairs were obvious and unsightly, prompting the courtiers to try and find a way of making the item look more attractive. Someone came up with the idea of mixing gold, silver or copper paste into the glue to make a feature of the repairs. They repaired what was broken rather than throwing it away or writing it off and did it in such a way that the restored item looked even more beautiful. As if the cracks were meant to be.

If your life were to develop cracks or fall apart I wonder what you might use to repair or restore it; how you might heal yourself?

You might find that you want to talk to someone: a trusted friend, maybe a counsellor or to people who can listen, such as the Samaritans. You might find that you want to do what I started doing: to write down exactly how you feel about a person, the world, the government, even God if you want to, and then tear it into pieces or burn it. You might prefer to express yourself artistically in painting, pottery, music, poetry, gardening or baking or through sport. You could also do this by kneading dough, bashing on drums, hitting a punch bag or trying to dig out stubborn roots or weeds as good ways of getting rid of frustration. Some people have started art journals which prove to be therapeutic.

Celine Santini has written a book called 'Kintsugi: Finding Strength in Imperfection.' It describes each stage of the Kintsugi process and how this might relate, or apply, to our lives. It's filled with inspirational quotes, suggestions that might help with the healing process (for example, jigsaw therapy) and space to write your own notes and record feelings.

As a Christian, I believe in Jesus who makes all things new.

It's sometimes said that Christianity isn't a religion but a relationship. That may be a cliché but I think it's true. Religion, to me, suggests our attempts to find God: going to and serving in the church, doing good deeds, trying our best to be good, living with a slight fear that God will punish us if we don't "get it right." Those things aren't wrong in themselves, but they won't get us closer to God. The Christian Gospel, however, is how, through Jesus, God made it possible for us to have a relationship with Him that's closer than that of a brother, good friend or even partner. It's a relationship that starts with and arises from God's unconditional love for us. It's a relationship that we can trust. God isn't remote, aloof, unable to empathise with us; He has shared our lives and walked in our shoes.

Are you homeless? So was Jesus. He understands.

Have you suffered pain, rejection, agony or bereavement? So has Jesus.

Have you wondered where God was, or questioned what He was doing? So has Jesus.

Do some people try and make you into the person they want you to be, belittle you as a person or what you stand for? They did that to Jesus too.

He can talk to God about us and on our behalf because He's been there. He was both God and man and He can mediate between both parties.

It might have taken only minutes to write the above paragraph but it took me a long time to discover the truth of it. I was once told that if I couldn't remember the exact date on which I became a Christian and received new life, I may not have done it. It wasn't a very encouraging statement at the time and it's not true. Relationships need time to grow and develop. When I was a teenager, my faith started to become real to me instead of theoretical and something I thought I had because I went to church. I heard the words that Jesus loved me and it has taken many years to be able to accept them and to explore a little of what that love means. I'm still learning: Jesus is still making me new. He is helping me to become the person He made me to be. What's more, I have the right to be the person He made me to be – we all have!

There are resources in the next section for anyone who would like to meet and get to know the man, Jesus. As well as these, Mark's Gospel, the shortest of the accounts of Jesus's life, is a good place to start. Or you might like to try a local church. I know what I've said about it, but that was largely about the church as an institution. A local, friendly accessible church is a good place to find out more about the faith and meet people who might have the same interests, experiences or questions as you. Some churches hold Alpha courses, where you can do all of the above and you get a free meal!

There is something else which is important in healing and reconciliation: forgiveness.

I have often struggled to understand forgiveness and I think that, generally, it is misunderstood. I have occasionally heard news stories involving rape or murder where the victims or relatives have offered forgiveness to the perpetrators and then, in the next breath, said they hope they are arrested or serve time in prison. How can that be? Doesn't forgiveness mean forgetting — dismissing the crime as though it doesn't matter and saying that they plan to carry on as usual?

I used to think so.

My understanding of forgiveness, now, is that of someone choosing not to hold another person's crime, thoughtless words, damaging actions and so on against them. Not to hold grudges or seek revenge. If Bill committed a crime (broke into Alf's house, for example) and stole from him, he'd deserve punishment. Alf would deserve justice and would also have a right to hope and fight for that justice. Forgiveness, on Alf's part, would mean him not lying awake at night plotting revenge for when Bill came out of jail or after he'd paid his fine. It would mean not bad-mouthing Bill for years afterwards because he'd once gone off the rails. It's also not deciding that Bill's punishment wasn't severe enough and he had a right to mete out his own justice.

We may not have severe crimes committed against us but thoughtless, unnecessary or cruel words and actions can be just as damaging and require forgiveness.

We might also be guilty of inflicting hurts on others. We can't always see someone else's scars, and our words or actions might be the barb that causes the wound to reopen.

I know this to be true of my life.

The annoying, demented wasps that have been buzzing round in my head might be swatted by forgiveness.

Forgiveness is necessary and can be offered, even if others are unaware of it. Someone may never know that you've forgiven them but you will. Forgiveness is healing, restoring and can set a person free – usually the one offering it. It's been said that unforgiveness can even cause physical problems. I've read of people with high blood pressure, ulcers and even arthritis which were caused, or worsened, by bitterness, anger and a lack of forgiveness. This doesn't mean that someone with an ulcer has it because they need to forgive.

The Bible characters that I've written about all received forgiveness: from others but also from the God who made them and whom they had let down. Simon Peter was adamant that he would never deny Jesus. Yet he did just that, swearing an oath and calling down curses on himself. Joseph forgave his eleven brothers who had tried to kill him, then sold him into slavery. We aren't told that Saul asked forgiveness from the Church. However, seeing as they accepted him and later came to value him as a dear brother, it's not impossible that he did so.

Ultimately, we can all be forgiven by God, who sent His Son to die for our sins. This means that God doesn't punish us by sending illness, unemployment, bereavement or any other awful event over our lives. He doesn't remember things that we did many years ago, neither does He bear grudges. A person who's been forgiven by God has been made new and becomes His child; a redeemed, restored, valued child of God. They become the person they were made to be.

In his Gospel, Luke tells us of the time when Simon the Pharisee had an uninvited dinner guest (Luke 7:36-50). The visitor was a woman who had "led a sinful life." She'd heard that Jesus would be at Simon's house and she wanted to see Him. In the society that Jesus lived in, women were second class citizens – or maybe not even as important as that. They had no rights, no education and no voice. They were unclean if they gave birth and doubly unclean if they gave birth to a girl. They were under their father's care until they were married, they became their husband's property and could be divorced by him for almost any reason.

So, it's an understatement to say that this woman was forward in marching, uninvited, into someone else's house. She ignored the social customs of the day and what other people would think because she wanted to see Jesus. When she saw Him, she began weeping, anointed Jesus's feet with her perfume and dried them with her hair. Simon was disgusted and seemed to assume that Jesus didn't know of the woman's sinful past, otherwise He wouldn't have let her touch Him. But Jesus told him a story of two men: one who'd been let off a debt of a few pounds and one who'd been let off a debt of thousands. Which one would love the most, Jesus asked. Simon supposed that it was the man who had owed the most money, which was the point that Jesus had wanted to make.

Simon had invited Jesus to share a meal with him. But he had not provided any water for his guest to wash his dusty feet, as was the custom. Nor had he given Jesus a customary kiss of greeting. It's almost like it was a casual, or maybe formal, relationship. Maybe Simon felt that he had to invite Jesus for a meal or did so to question Him, but that he didn't respect Him. It seems that the woman, on the other hand, had received forgiveness and acceptance from Jesus. So she sought Him out and expressed her love and gratitude. She knew she hadn't only been noticed, affirmed and restored, but forgiven, too.

Jesus can still do that for us today.

And that is why I've written this book.

Thank you for reading.

God bless,

Gill

It was though I had received new insight, clarity, new life.

Chapter 12
Saul's Story

My name is Saul and I'm very happy to tell you the story of how Jesus made me new.

I'm from Tarsus, which was a city in ancient Cilicia, known for its school of learning.

I'm from the Hebrew tribe of Benjamin but being from Tarsus, I was also granted Roman citizenship. I grew up in the Jewish faith and loved to learn about the history of my people, starting with Abraham, who had been promised that he would have many descendants and fathered his first child aged one hundred. Our history continued with his son, Isaac, and grandson, Jacob; all of whom became our patriarchs. As a boy, I loved to hear how Moses rescued our people from Egypt and caused the sea itself to part so that they could get through safely and escape from evil Pharaoh. I learnt about how he gave his law to the people that he had rescue and how we, of all nations on earth, are bound to God in a covenant. I learned God's law in the Torah, and also our oral law. I was a good student and studied under one of the best Rabbis by the name of Gamaliel.

I later became a Pharisee and enjoyed teaching the law to others and instructing them how to live as God's chosen people. I believe I was good at it.

I was very zealous for my faith.

I began hearing stories of a man from Nazareth: Jesus, son of Joseph, who was going around teaching about

God. He had twelve close followers and a few others who were calling Him Rabbi.

Rabbi means teacher and almost anyone can call himself that. But this man was teaching about God and I wasn't sure if He was qualified to be able to do that. Some of the things that He said, and did, sounded pretty outrageous and He clashed with some of my peers who, quite rightly, criticised Him for working on the Sabbath and not obeying some of the finer points of the law. Anyone who says that they're teaching about God needs to teach the truth. The Lord, or YHWH (His name is too sacred for a Jew to say, or even to write) is Holy, pure, perfect and commands respect. But this man was calling Him Abba, a very informal word, and talking to Him as though they were best mates. It was all rather disturbing. I also heard that He forgave people their sins and, somehow, made unclean people clean again. Now that wasn't on. True, He did usually tell the person to show themselves to the priest, so He was obviously aware of the correct procedure. But forgiving sins? No one can do that except God.

I admit that I don't know how He managed to make sick people well again, which was a good thing to do. But He did, somehow, and many people started to speak well about this lawbreaker and to follow Him.

Something had to be done about this.

It wasn't long before I heard that something had been done: Jesus had been arrested. He was, rightly, accused of blasphemy and had even stated that if someone should pull down the temple, He would rebuild it in three days. There was a trial and His supporters tried to claim that it was illegal because it was held at night, but I'm sure the chief priests and elders knew what they were doing. At any rate, they found Jesus guilty and He was eventually sentenced to be crucified.

And that was that: another false Messiah gone. Another blasphemer and enemy of our glorious faith, taken care of. A pity, in one way, as I'd heard that Jesus had done great things and helped many. But we cannot let our God-given faith be sullied by a few good deeds. No, whatever movement this imposter had come to start, was over.

But then I began to hear alarming news: His followers were claiming that Jesus was alive again and they'd seen Him. Others were being taken in by these claims.

Outrageous! Impossible!

It was utterly impossible that anyone could come back to life. I mean, not that anyone would believe the stories. Sadly, there are people who are easily taken in and willing to believe anything. If God were ever to bring anyone back to life it would be someone worthy, someone who deserved another chance, not a deluded, blasphemous liar.

I don't know what tricks these followers (I don't like to use the word "Jews") used to try to persuade people to believe this story. Or maybe it wasn't a trick at all; maybe they went to the wrong tomb. Maybe they themselves even moved the body so that they could make it look as though this Jesus had done what He was going to do. Yes, that sounds about right. Well, that could be easily solved, I thought. All we had to do was forbid the followers from spreading this nonsense; imprison them, devise some punishment and go in hard. They would soon crumble and admit the truth. They were just a bunch of fishermen. They wouldn't be brave enough to stand against opposition; look how they all ran away and hid when Jesus was arrested!

I heard that someone had been arrested; not one of the original followers but another guy called Stephen who'd been appointed as some kind of leader in their group. He was accused of criticising Moses and speaking against the temple and the law. Some teachers of the law had heard him say that Jesus, who was now alive, had spoken against Moses.

To be fair, I heard that Stephen gave a very impressive speech and courageous defence. I heard that his speech drew on and appealed to our history; facts that no one would have been able to contradict. This might have persuaded some that he wasn't as opposed to Moses as they'd thought. But it was his accusation that they, the elite Jewish leaders and Sanhedrin, had murdered God's righteous and chosen One, that really sealed his fate. The punishment for blasphemy was stoning to death, according to our law. So that's what they did. They asked me to hold their cloaks as they did so as they needed to be able to move freely when they picked up and threw the rocks.

It wasn't so much the stoning that shook me (it wasn't pleasant) but we were obeying the law and getting rid of a blasphemer. It was the way that he died. He didn't retract his words or his beliefs when he saw them picking up the jagged rocks. He neither changed his mind, nor called down curses as they fell. Quite the opposite – he asked that the Lord would forgive them.

I'd been certain that any follower of Jesus would buckle under pressure, change their minds and stories, confess that they were mistaken. Not only did Stephen stick to his story, but he also prayed for those who opposed him, even as they carried out the death sentence. What's more, people were still signing up to become followers of the Way, in spite of what could happen to them! I didn't mind if Gentiles wanted to follow a false Messiah, but even our people were falling for this nonsense.

I didn't have time to wonder about that nor about Stephen, however. We were told we needed to crack down hard on these people and I was doing all I could to get these heretics into prison.

I wanted to go to Damascus and arrest any that I found there, and I got letters of authorisation from the High Priest which would've allowed me to do just that.

I set off and was nearly at Damascus when I suddenly saw a bright light in the sky; not the sun, it was way too bright for that. It startled and blinded me. It could only have been the light of God; far purer and brighter than natural light. I fell to the ground and heard a voice asking why I was persecuting Him.

"Who are you Lord?"

"I am Jesus, whom you are persecuting," was the reply. "Now get up and go into the city."

I was speechless.

The Lord was *Jesus* and I was persecuting *Him*?

When I opened my eyes, I found that I was blind as well; I could see nothing. But even if I'd been able to see, I would still have been in darkness. Everything I thought I knew was suddenly in question.

Jesus of Nazareth, our Messiah? How was that even possible?

I was without my sight for a while and didn't eat or drink during that time – I was in shock. Then I had a vision that a man would come, lay his hands on me and I'd see again. And it was so. It was as though I had scales on my eyes, which suddenly fell off. It was though I had received new insight, clarity, new life. My sight was restored on the third day.

I went straight to the believers in Damascus, not to arrest them, but to share what had happened and to find out more about Jesus.

I now knew that He was the Messiah and told anyone who would listen. They were suspicious of me. Of course they were. I could've been undercover to get information. I might have been going to have them killed (my reputation had preceded me). They could also have turned on me and try to have me killed. In fact, the only people who tried to do that were my fellow Jews. These followers of the Way, former enemies of mine, helped me to escape.

I wanted to stay in Damascus for as long as possible to tell people about Jesus and how He had turned my life around. But I still needed to process this properly and work out whether this new revelation supplanted, contradicted or somehow completed my Jewish faith. So, I went off to Arabia for a few years to work it all out so that I could give answers to anyone who asked.

They did ask. They questioned, argued, debated and disagreed.

That was quite understandable; after all, I was asking Jews to believe that their Messiah had already come and they'd failed to recognise it and then killed Him. I didn't mind debates and arguments. I didn't even mind that they doubted or questioned my experience on the road to Damascus.

What I did mind was when people distorted what I was saying and this new faith.

Although I debated with Jews, I was called and sent mainly to proclaim Jesus to the Gentiles. Gentiles are people who are not Jews – that's a polite name for them. Because they aren't God's people, they are thought to be unclean, outside of God's promises and also His love. Now, I was being asked to go and tell them that Jesus was for them also; that He could forgive and take their sins from them and they, too, could become God's children and His chosen.

Not everyone liked that thought.

Some seemed to accept it but tried to add to the Good News and lay down conditions: "Yes, Jesus died for you, but to be fully accepted as God's children, you also have to be circumcised. Just as all God's people have had to be circumcised" (Men only, obviously!).

This is not true and not acceptable and I told them so in no uncertain terms.

The Good News is that God created all people in His image, accepts and loves all people and that Jesus died for all people. We can't add to that.

Jews were called to be God's people, chosen to help Gentiles find God. When Jesus came, it became possible for everyone to find God.

I began to receive physical threats and beatings because of the message that I was proclaiming. Some Jews didn't like hearing that they had killed the Messiah; some didn't like, or believe, that Jesus had been raised to life again. Some didn't want Gentiles to hear this message. Some Gentiles believed that they were being told that their gods were false.

I understood it.

No one wants to be challenged about their deep held beliefs; to find that they've devoted their lives to something which isn't, in fact, true. People don't want to be told that the possession, or maybe tradition, that they treasure most has no power to help them. So, I was physically injured on more than one occasion: flogged, stoned, imprisoned, shipwrecked and in danger from Jews and Gentiles alike. This didn't stop me from proclaiming the message, however. I went on several journeys and founded churches along the way. I felt responsible for these communities of new believers. It was great to visit, encourage them and watch them grow into mature, confident Christians. Though some of the churches gave me a headache – just as much as the unbelievers who opposed me.

It was ironic that I, who had been one of the chief persecutors, throwing people into prison without another thought because they disagreed with my faith, was now being persecuted and flung into prison when people disliked what I said.

I sometimes wonder if I didn't persecute the believers because I was fearful; fearful because they were joyful, assured, bold and had the kind of relationship with God that I had always wanted. Maybe I was fearful because the very fact of their changed lives (from cowards to champions of their faith) and their actions as miracle workers might mean that there was something in their claims. Was there a tiny part of me, a small, buried voice that was saying that their words might be true?

I wonder if people persecute me out of fear; fear that I might lose them money, power, authority. Maybe they persecute me out of fear that they might have to re-examine some long-held beliefs and maybe change. If only they knew that Jesus could set us free from fear and from anything else that keeps us in chains.

I am in chains now, as I write. I wouldn't be surprised if this time they do silence me for good. But the Gospel isn't in chains and cannot be silenced. Death isn't the end; it's the beginning of a life with Him, forever. We are freed from our worn out bodies. We are free from pain, death, disease, temptations, weaknesses and all the other things that get in the way and stop us from being the people He made us to be.

I may die soon, but you, who are reading this, are still alive. However many bad things you have done in your life, there is hope.

GILL TAGGART

About the Author

I am a full-time volunteer and a lay preacher in the Methodist Church. I like to use creative arts in leading worship and am interested in using many of these arts as therapy. I enjoy crafts, gardening and music and live in Cheshire with two cats and my husband.

I am not yet the person that God made me to be; I am still learning.

GILL TAGGART

Resources Page

These are a few resources that you might find helpful. Some of these have been referenced in the book.

Chapter 1

Compassionate Friends – www.tcf.org.uk
Cruse – www.cruse.org.uk
Rainbow Trust – www.rainbowtrust.org.uk

Chapter 2

Insight into addiction by Bill Radmall
Pub by CWR
For short, online course on this and other subjects, go to:
www.waverleyabbeycollege.ac.uk/

Chapter 9

ME www.meassociation.org.uk
www.actionforme.org.uk

A Way through the Wilderness
Jamie Buckingham
Risky Living Ministries inc 2013

Chapter 10

Dementia
www.alzheimers.org.uk , www.dementiauk.org

Chapter 11

Books on restoration:

Kintsugi: Finding Strength in Imperfection.
Celine Santini
Andrews McMeel Publishing 2019

Restoring the Fallen
Mark and Cherith Stibbe
Mark uses the picture of Kintsugi to show how his, once broken, life was restored.
Malcolm Down Publishing March 2019

Art Journals and Creative Healing:

Restoring the Spirit through Creative Expression
Sharon Soneff
Quarry books 2008

The Creative Arts in Dementia Care
Jill Hayes with Sarah Povey
Jessica Kingsley Publishers 2011

The Christian Faith

Christianity
https://christianity.org.uk

Christianity Explored
https://www.christianityexplored.org

Church Army
https://churcharmy.org

Printed in Great Britain
by Amazon